tweets from the dog™

#happytails

written by Miki Klocke and Mary Ogle
photography by Miki Klocke

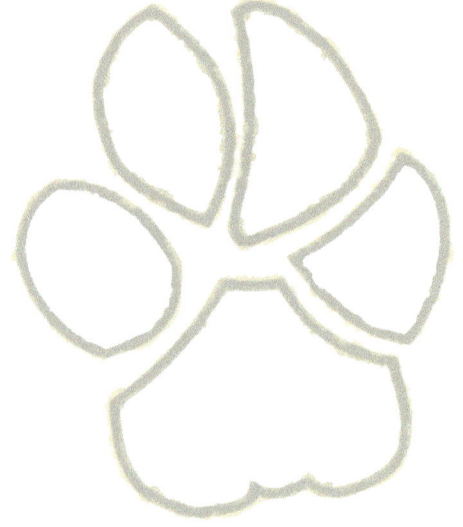

Copyright © 2016 by Miki Klocke and Mary Ogle
All rights reserved. This book or any portion thereof may not be reproduced or used in any manner whatsoever without the express written
permission of Miki Klocke and Mary Ogle except for the use of brief quotations in a book review.

Printed in the United States of America

First Printing, 2016

ISBN: 978-1541192348

Miki Klocke and Mary Ogle
mikiandmary@wordandpicturebook.com
wordandpicturebook.com

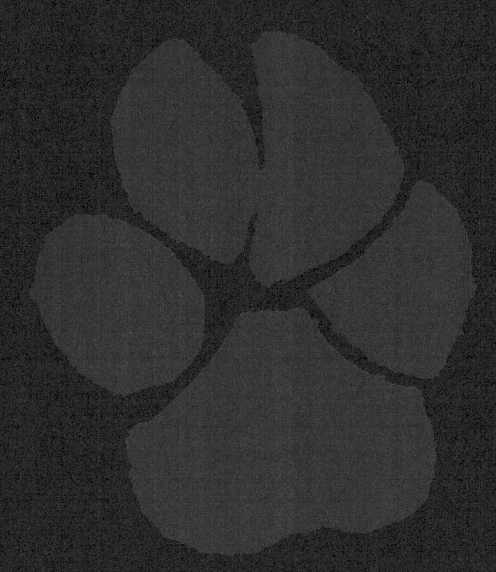

Dedicated to
Moose and Hugo

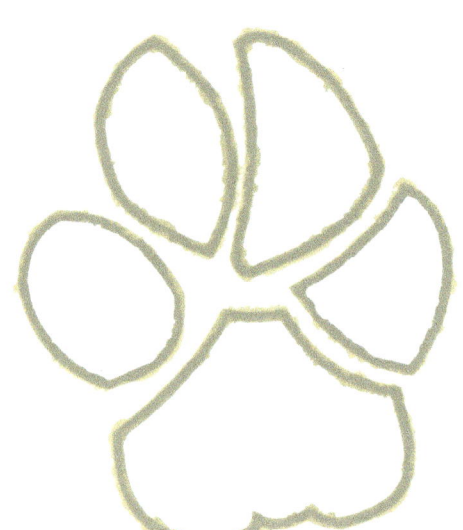

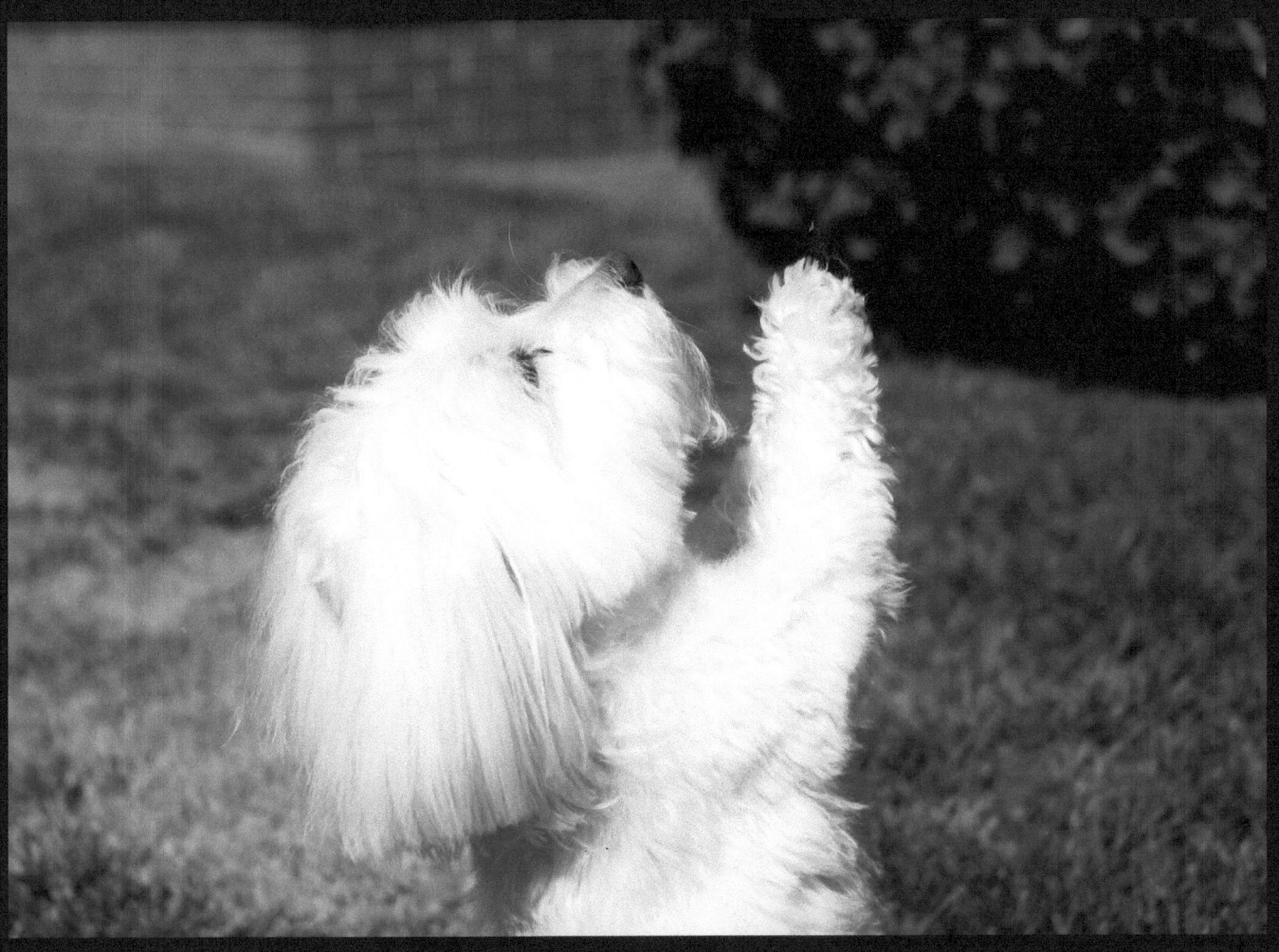

Every day I wake up and thank dog.
#howlalujah

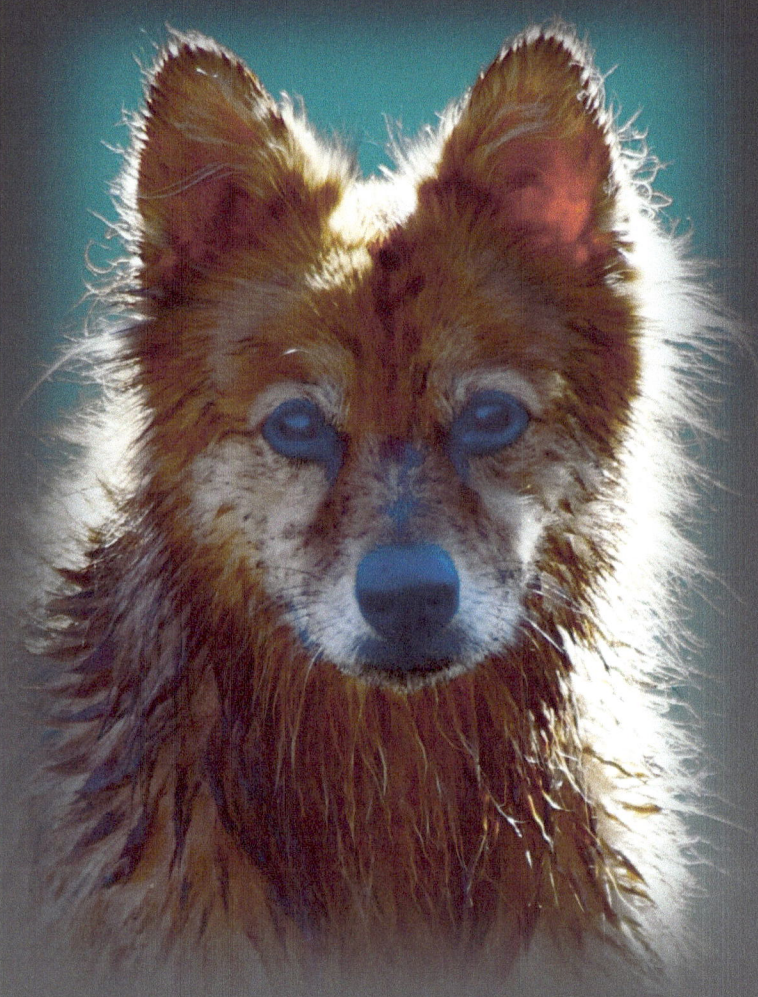

Your dog loves you. Your wet dog loves you more.
#dirtydog

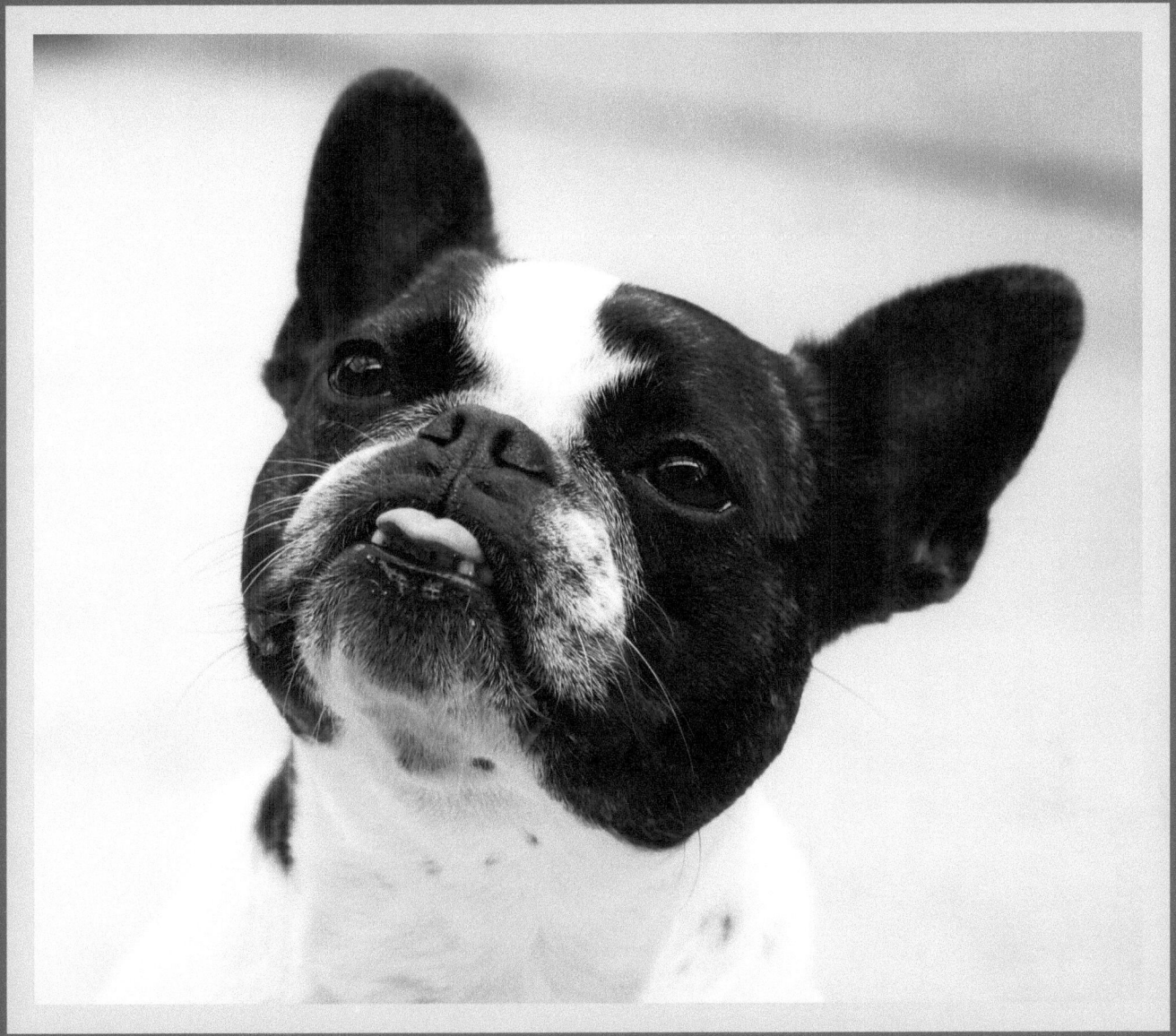

You can't start the party without the licker.
#pupapalooza

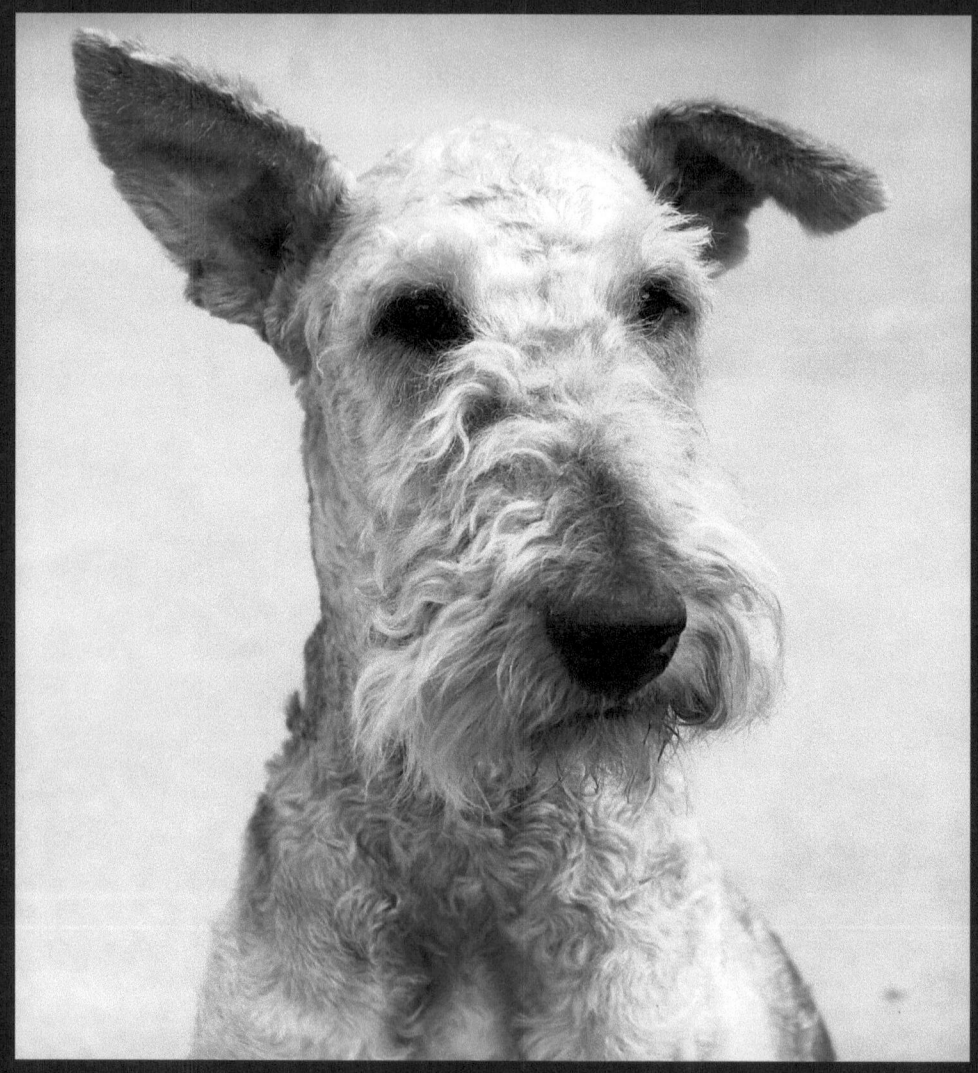

It's not a good day unless you smell at the end of it.
#stinkbomb

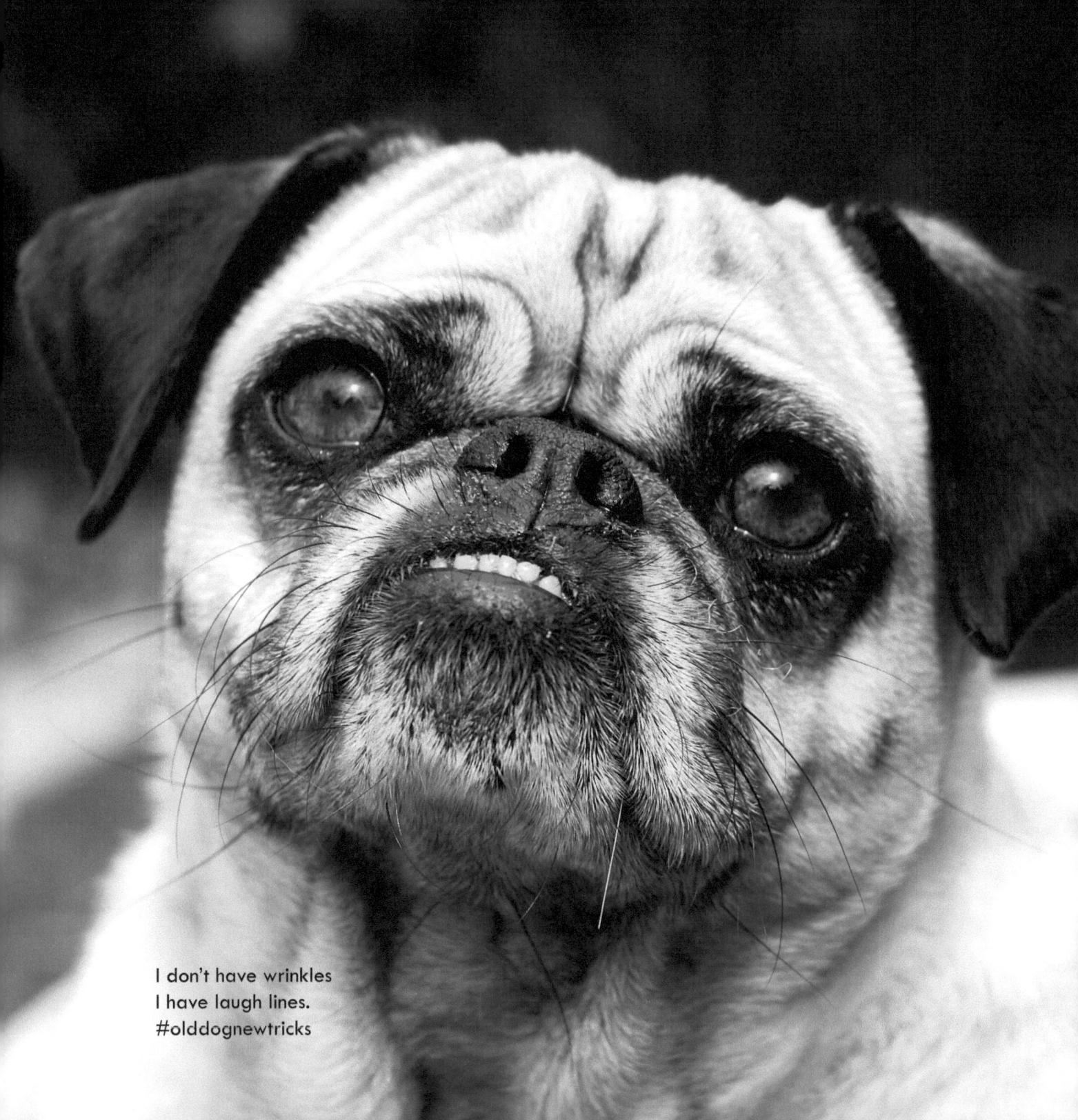

I don't have wrinkles
I have laugh lines.
#olddognewtricks

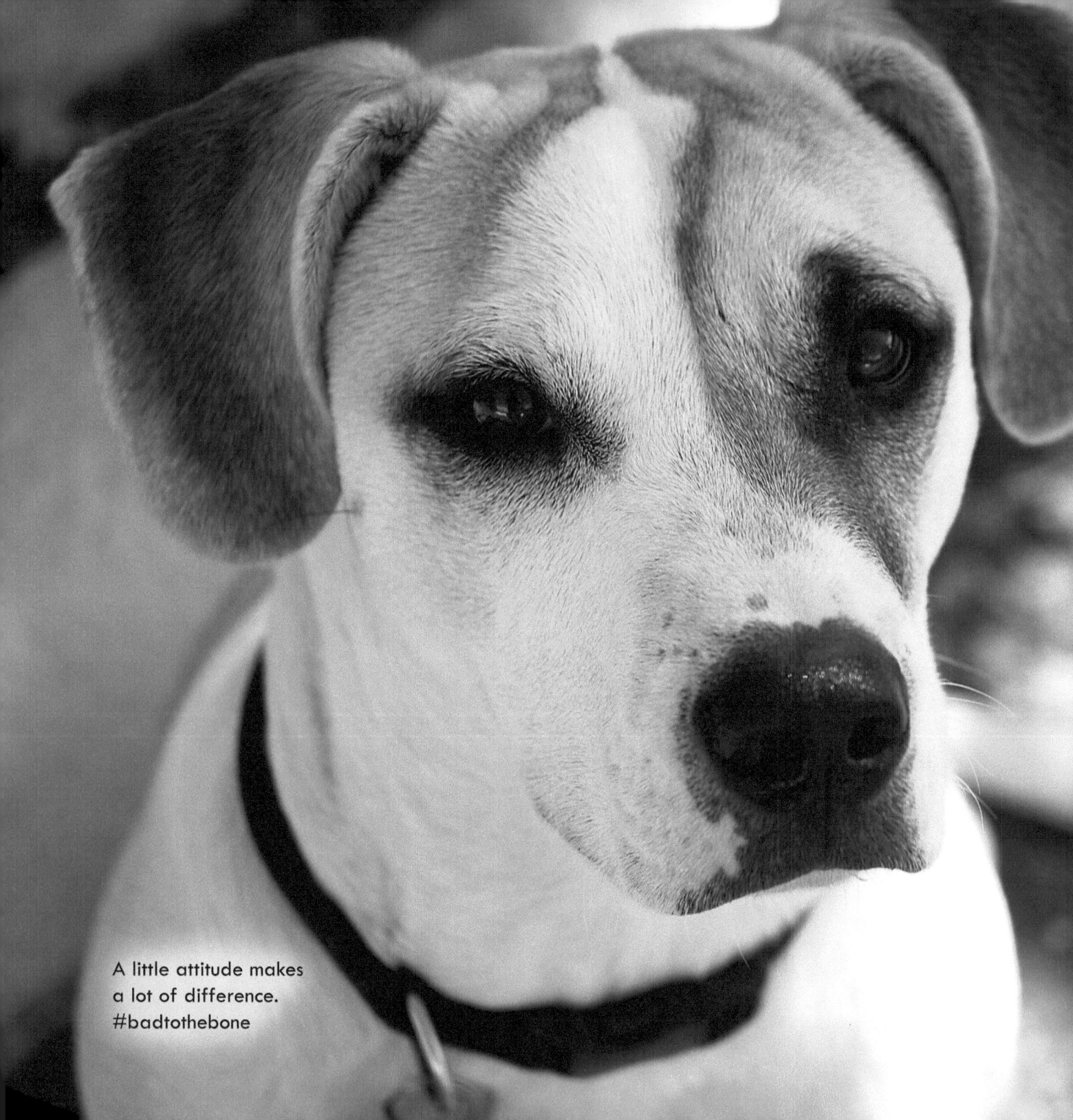

A little attitude makes
a lot of difference.
#badtothebone

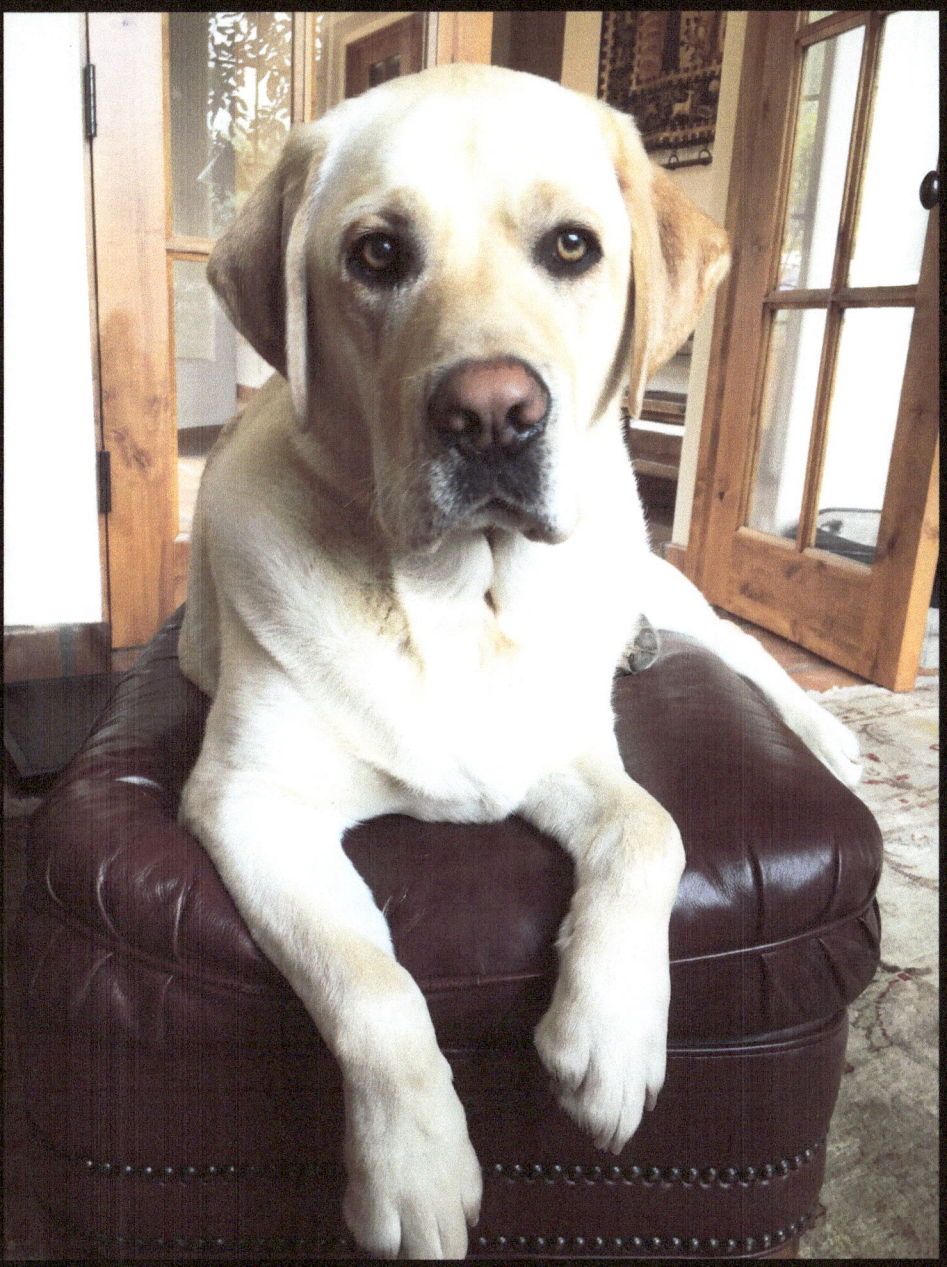

When they think you're too big to sit in their lap block their view of the tv.
#iwin

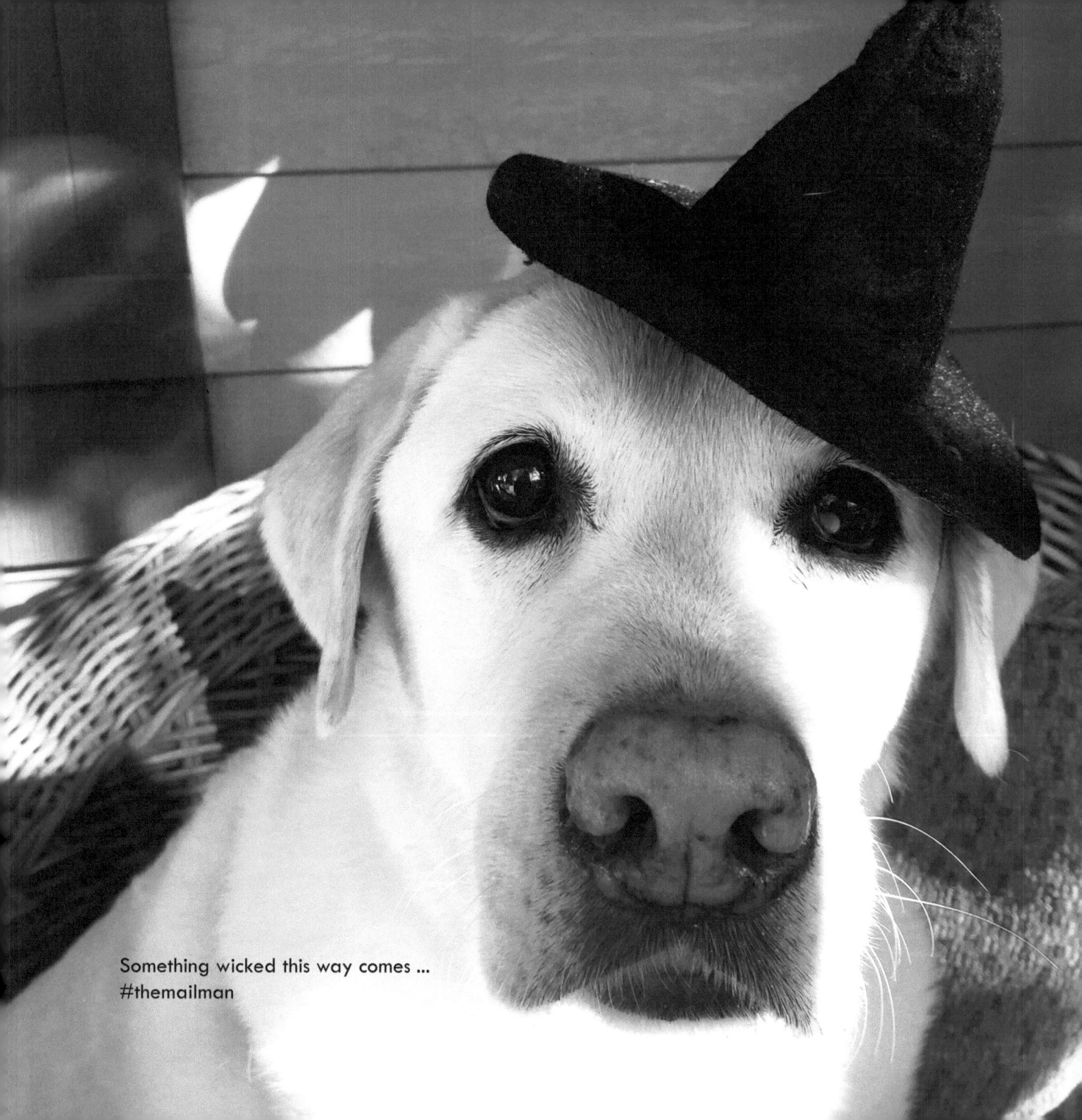

Something wicked this way comes ...
#themailman

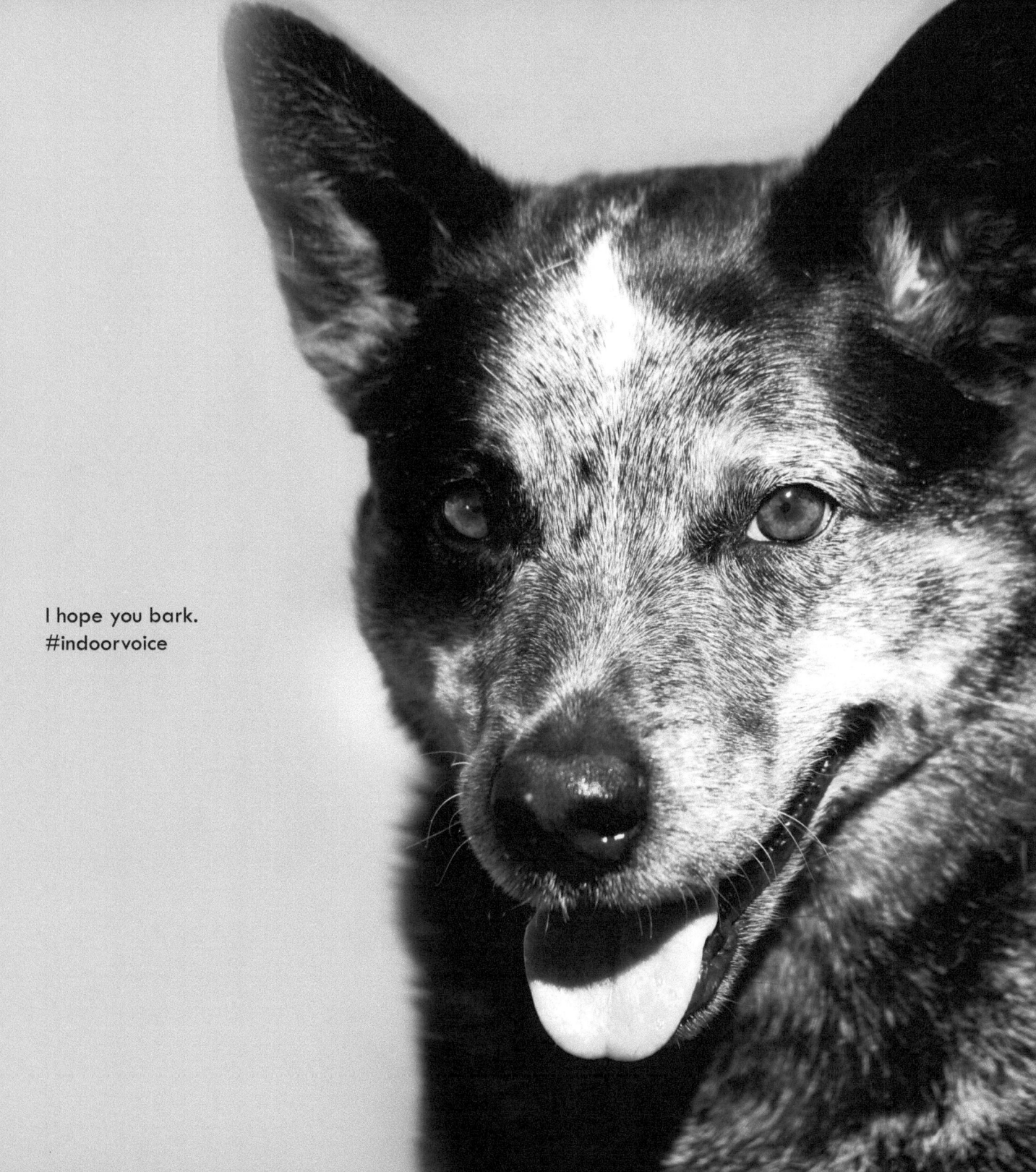

I hope you bark.
#indoorvoice

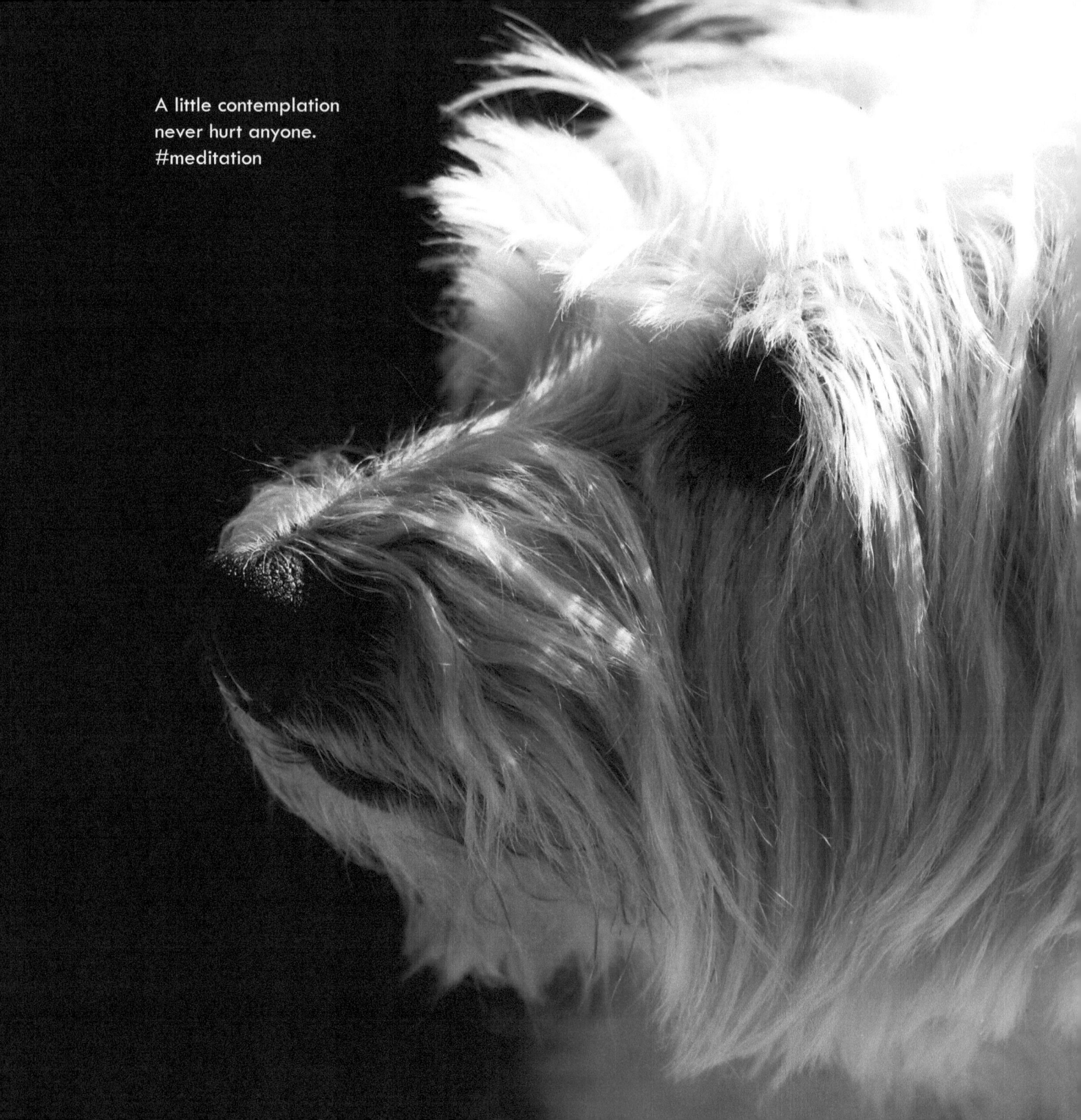

A little contemplation
never hurt anyone.
#meditation

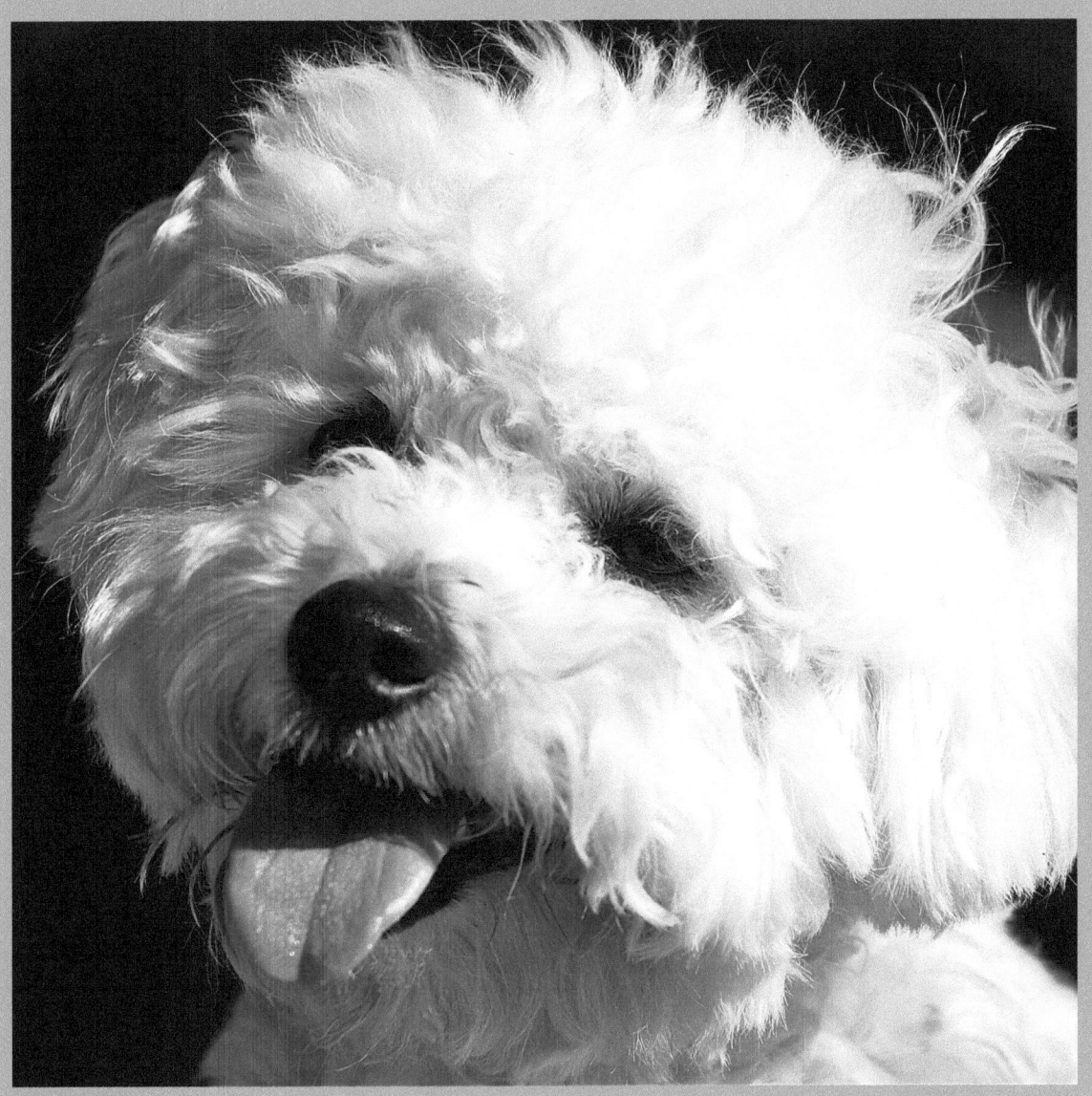

Smile at your dog and the world smiles back.
#dontworrybefurry

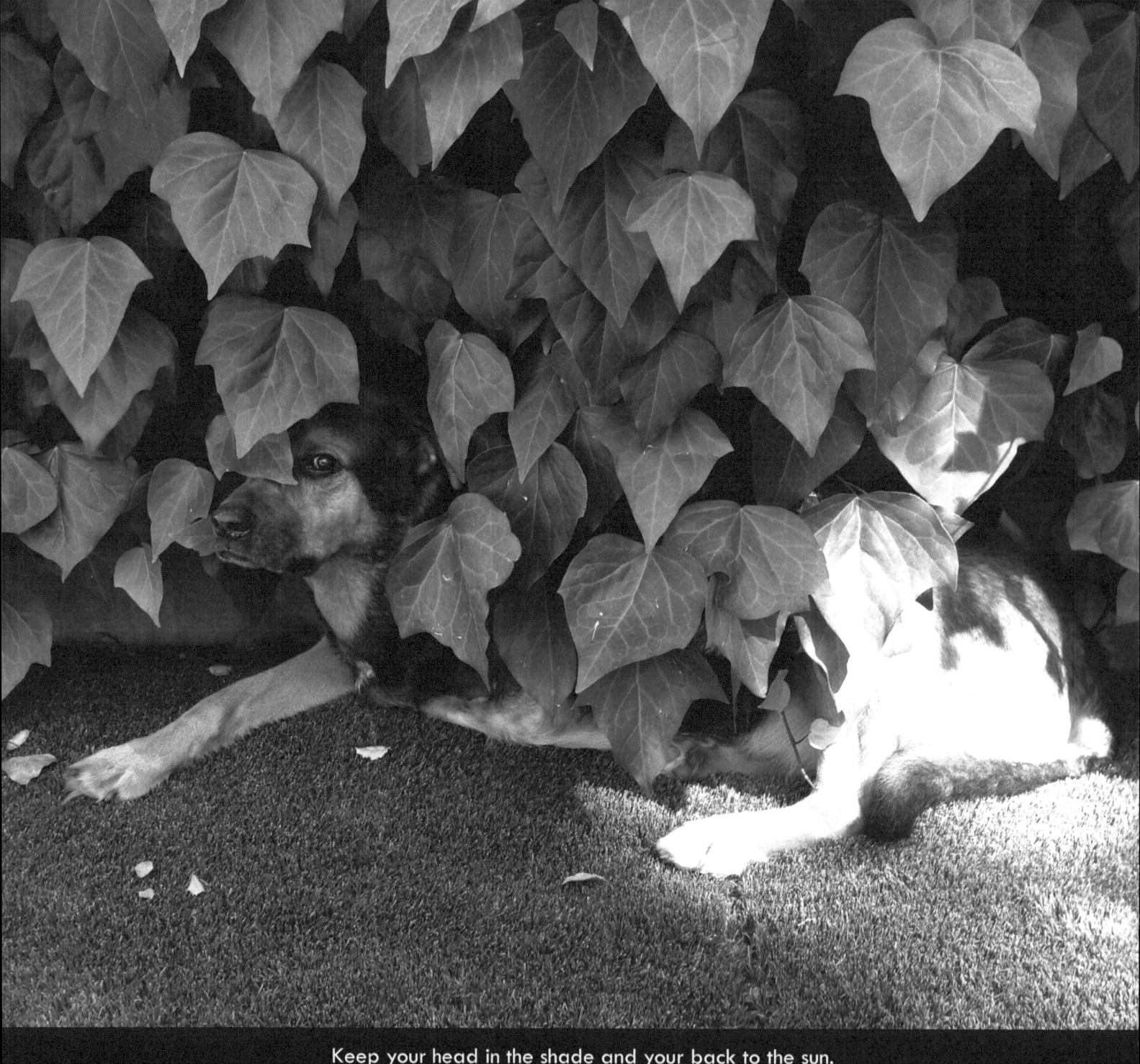

Keep your head in the shade and your back to the sun.
#seriously

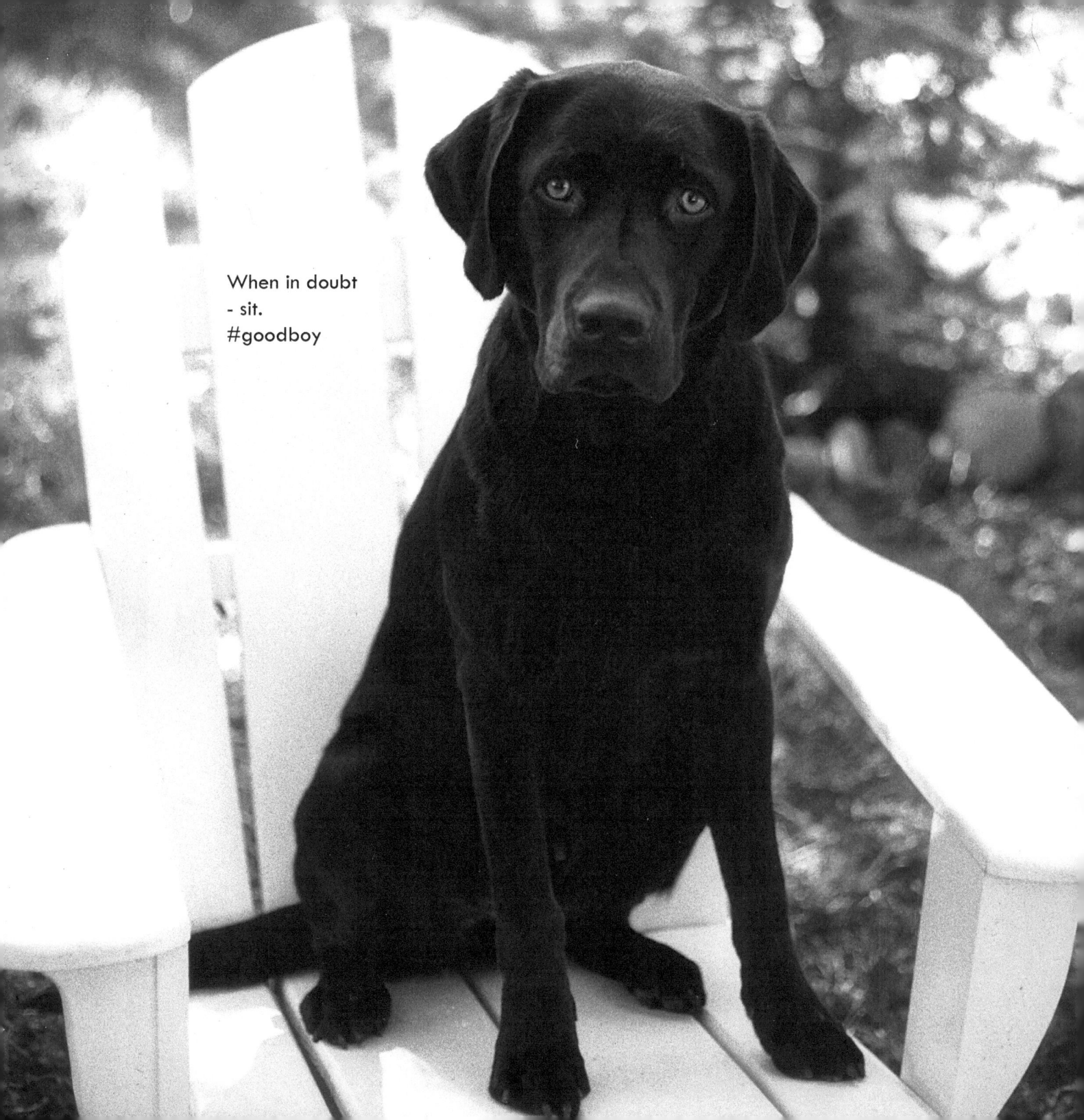

When in doubt
- sit.
#goodboy

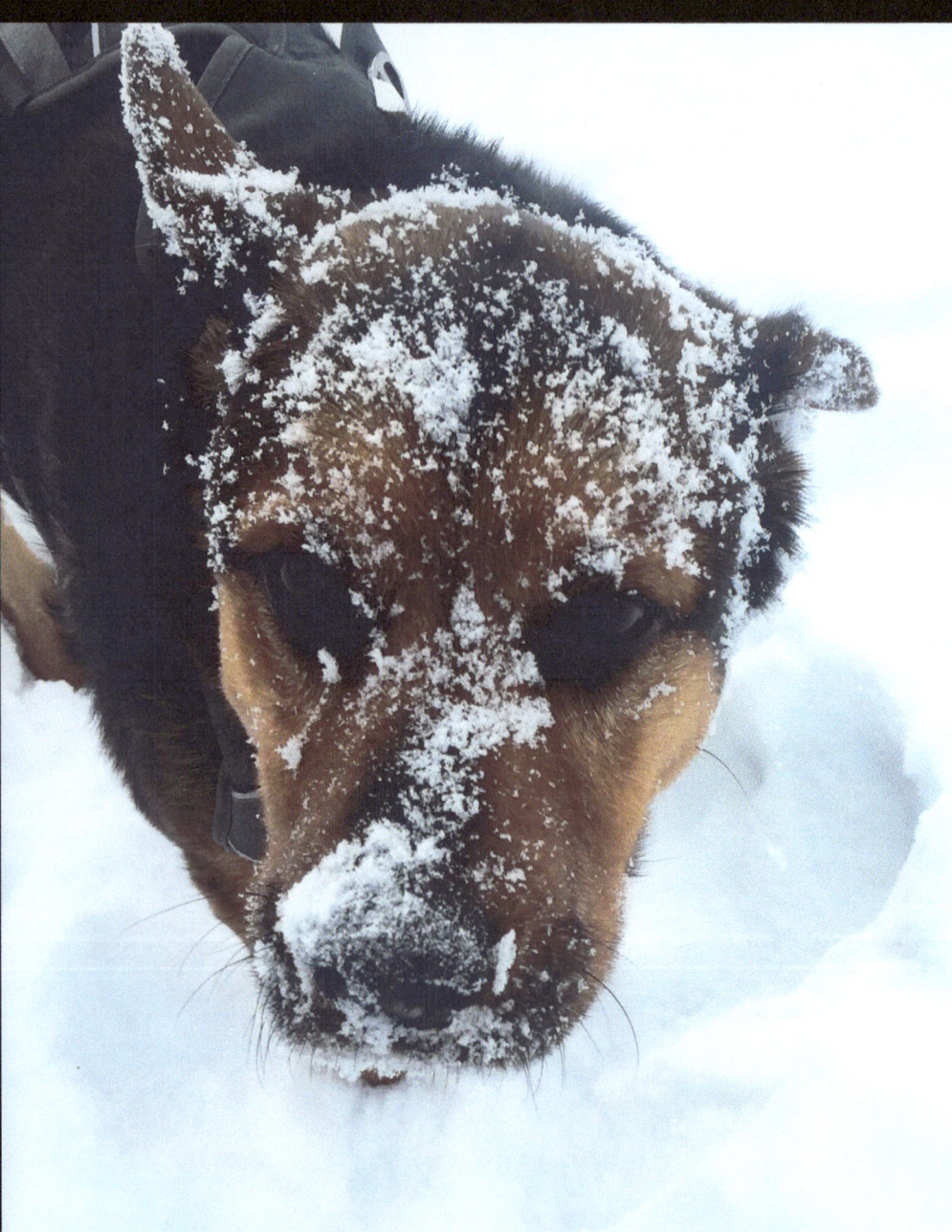

I know I left my toy out here somewhere.
#searchandrescue

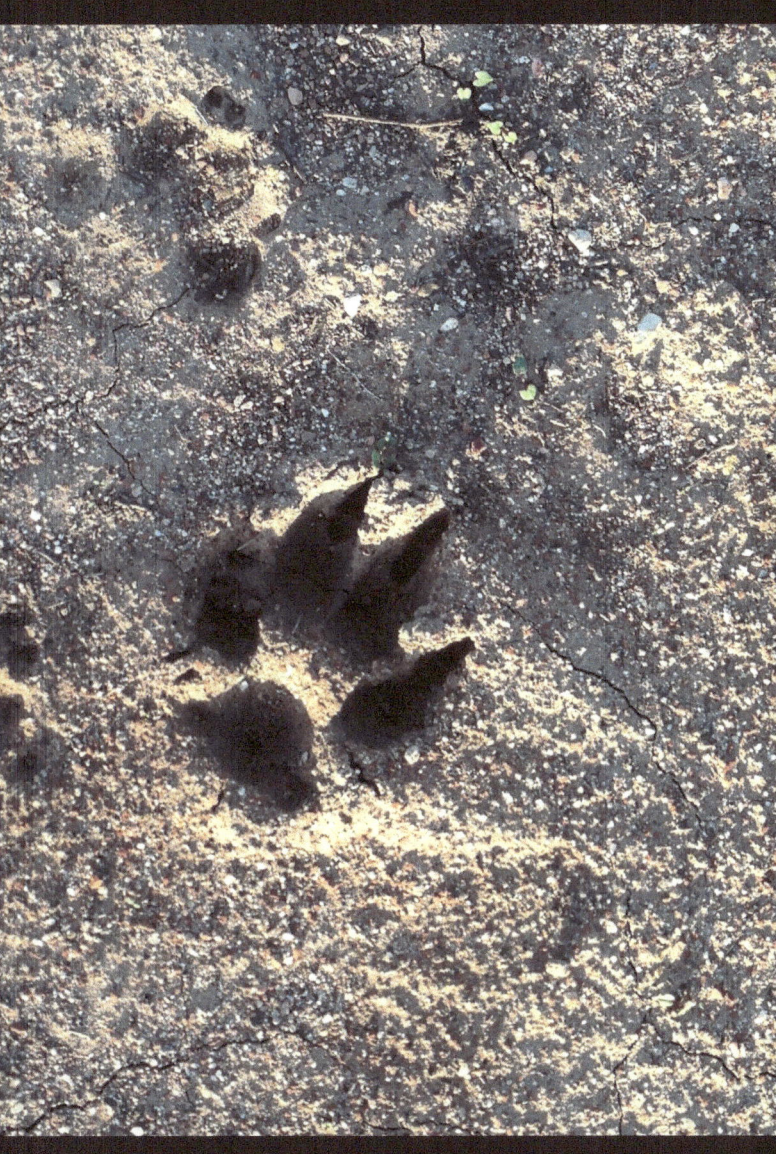

Dig in the sand but don't pee in the wind.
#leavepawprints

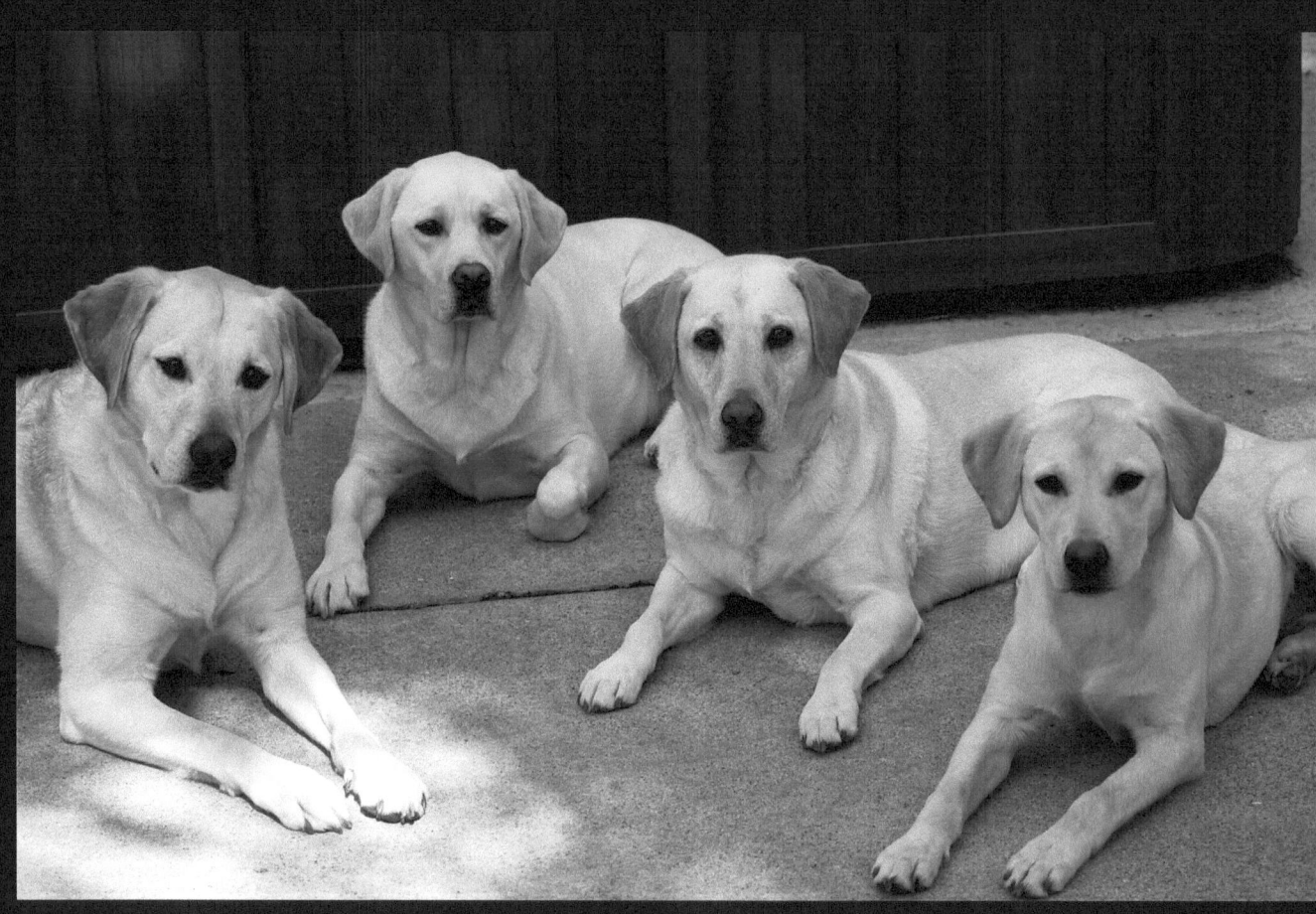

One is never enough.
#bounty

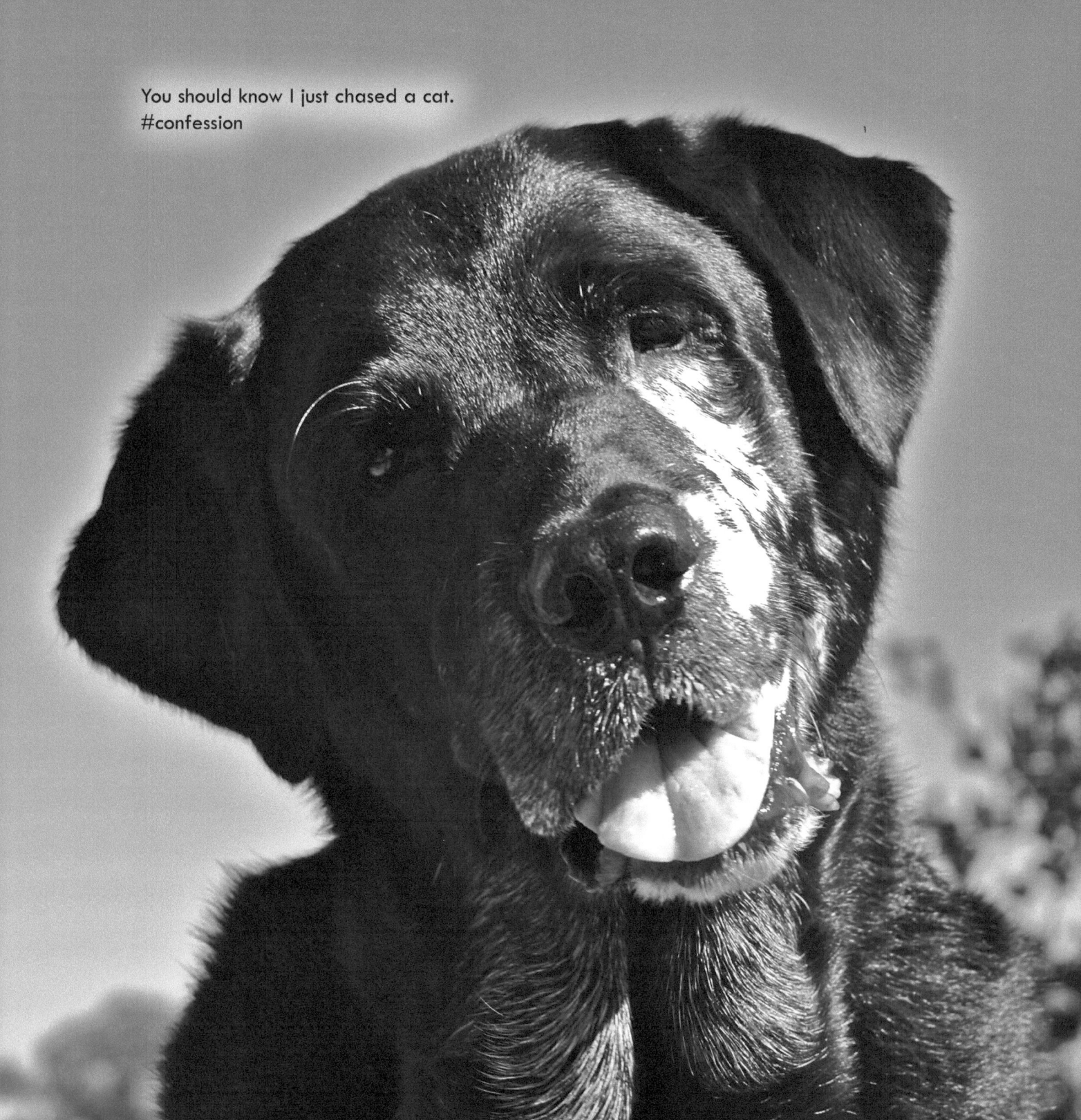

You should know I just chased a cat.
#confession

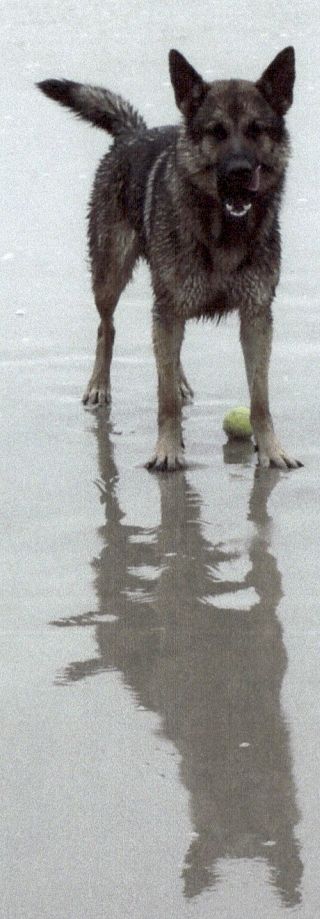

I'm so smart I trained my shadow to throw the ball.
#intelligent

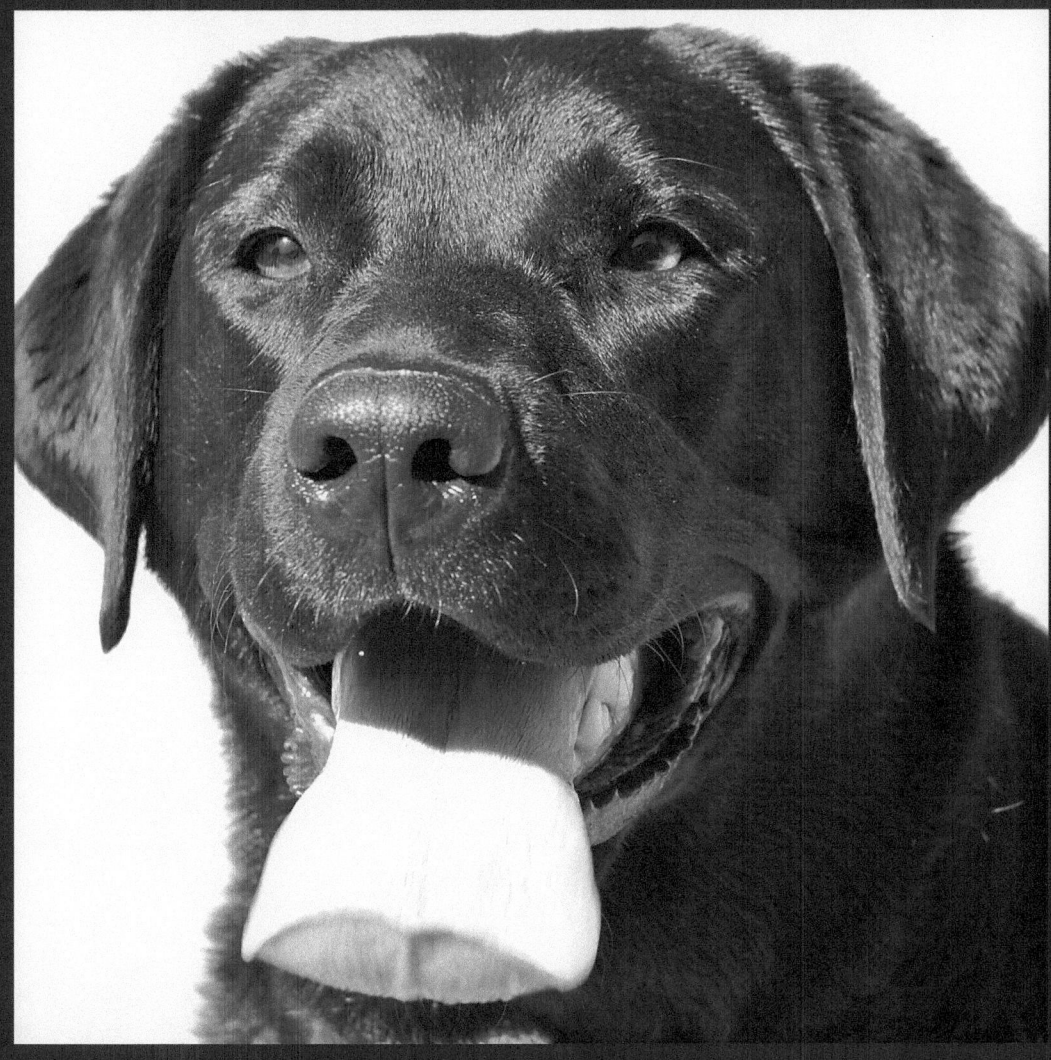

I recommend the merlot.
#whine

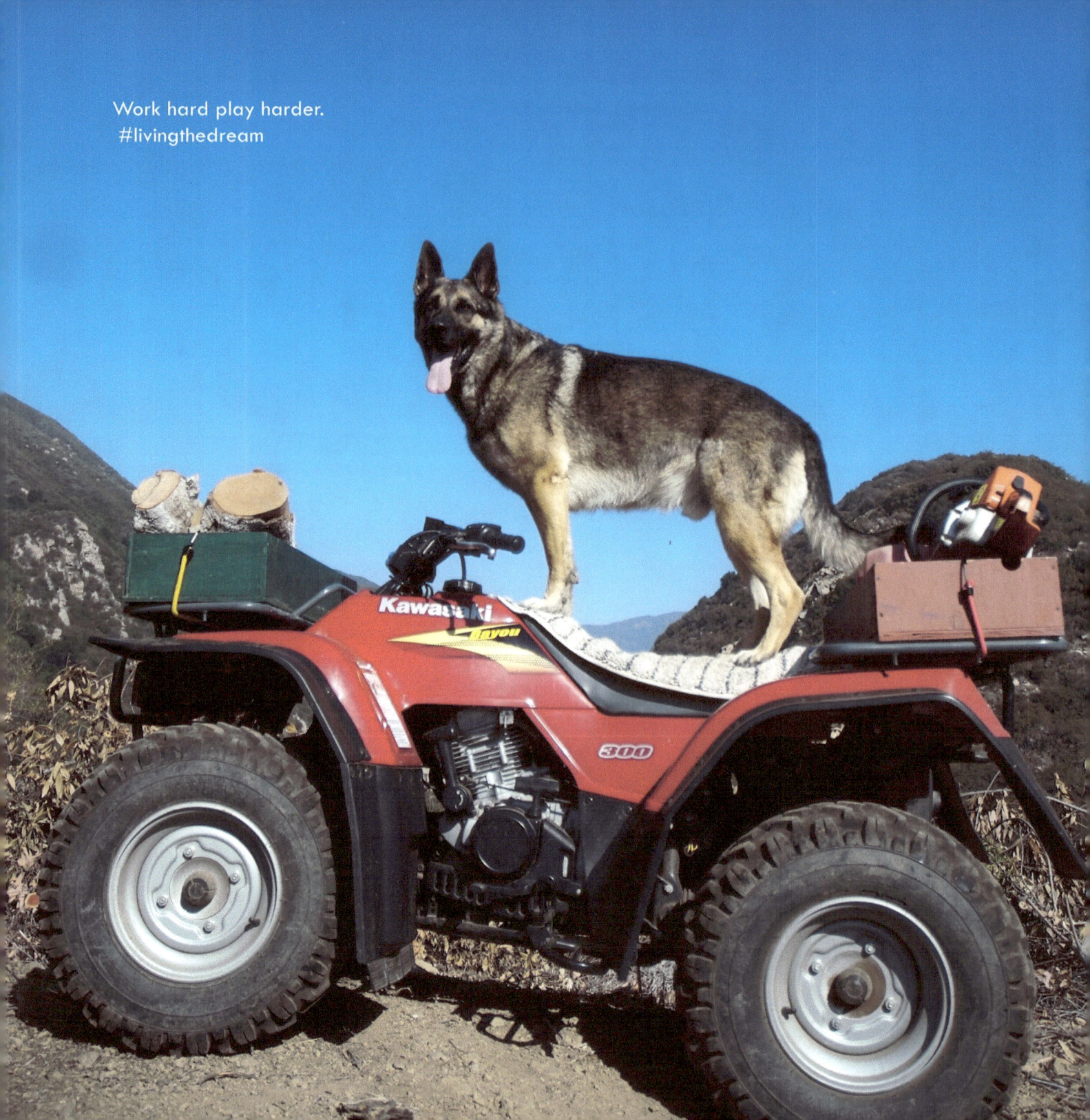

Work hard play harder.
#livingthedream

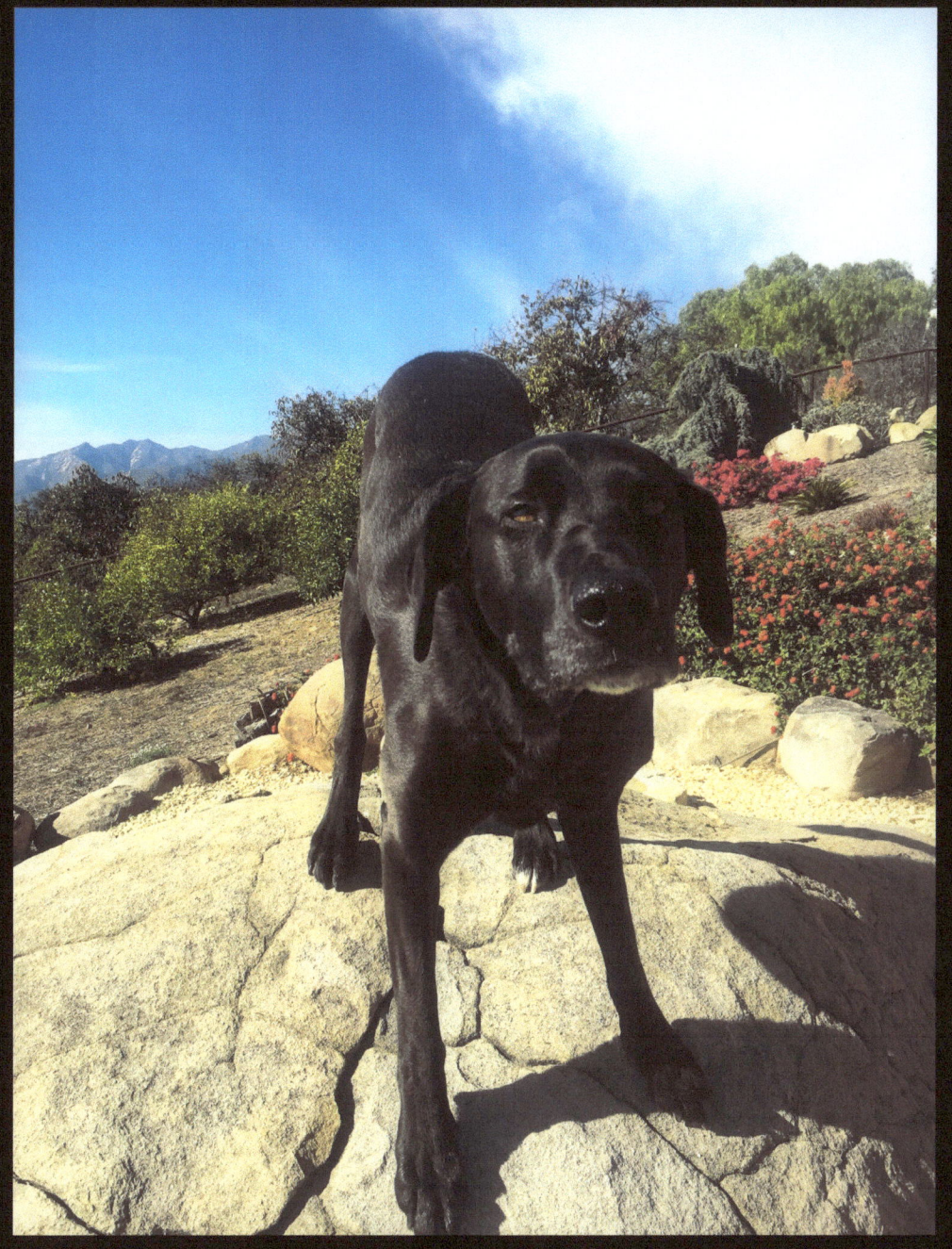

Play in the sunshine, sniff the wild air.

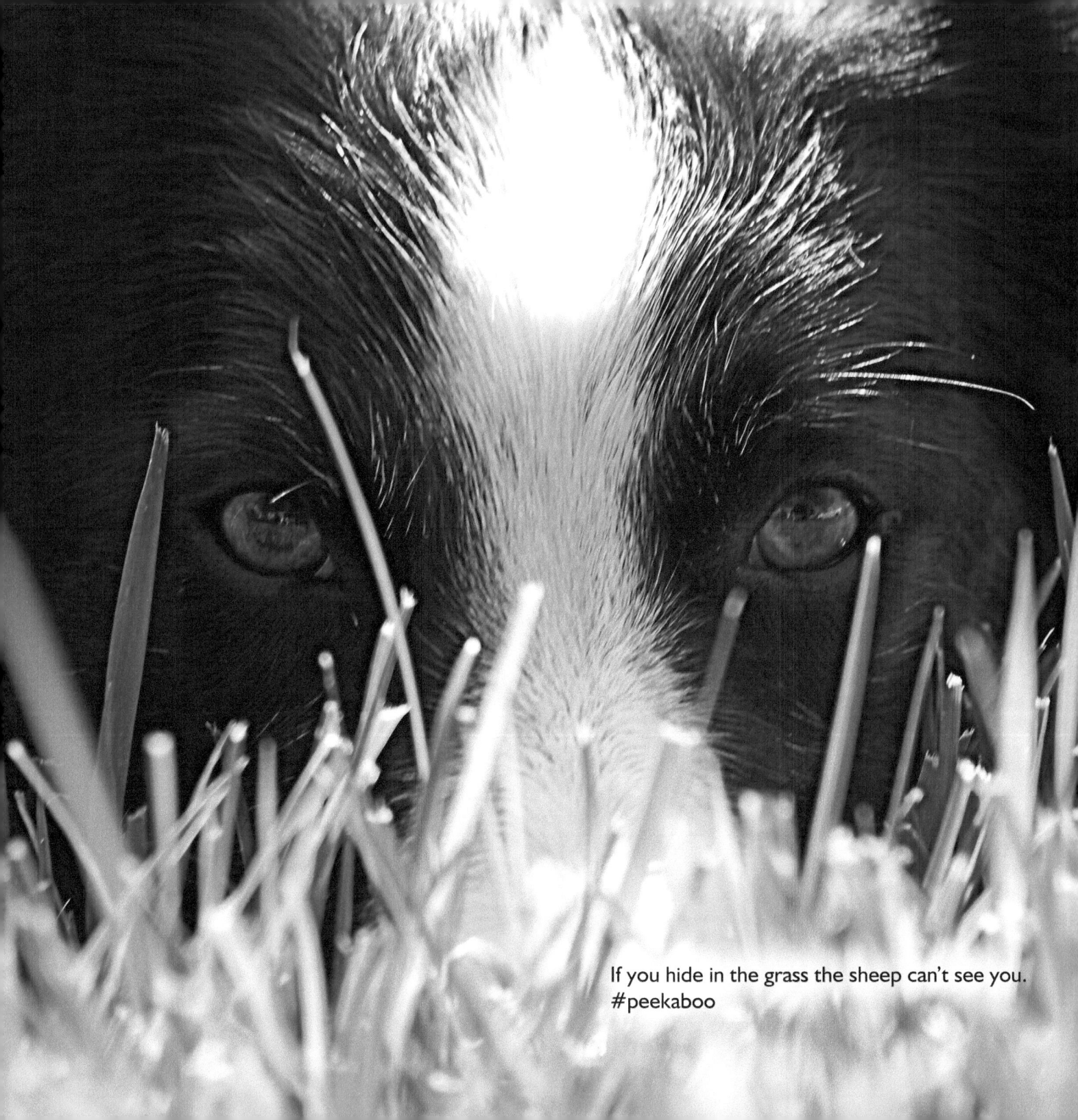

If you hide in the grass the sheep can't see you.
#peekaboo

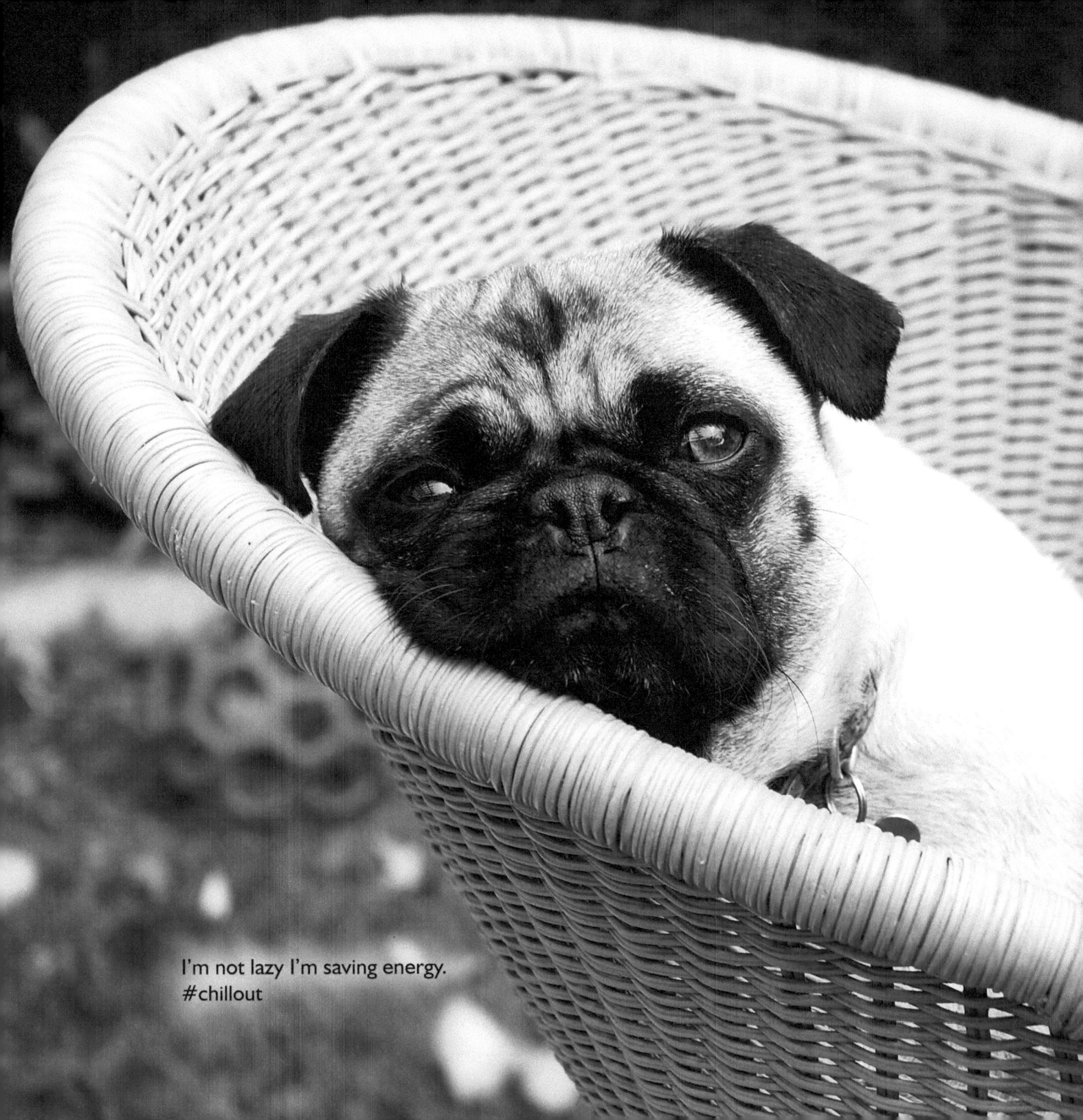

I'm not lazy I'm saving energy.
#chillout

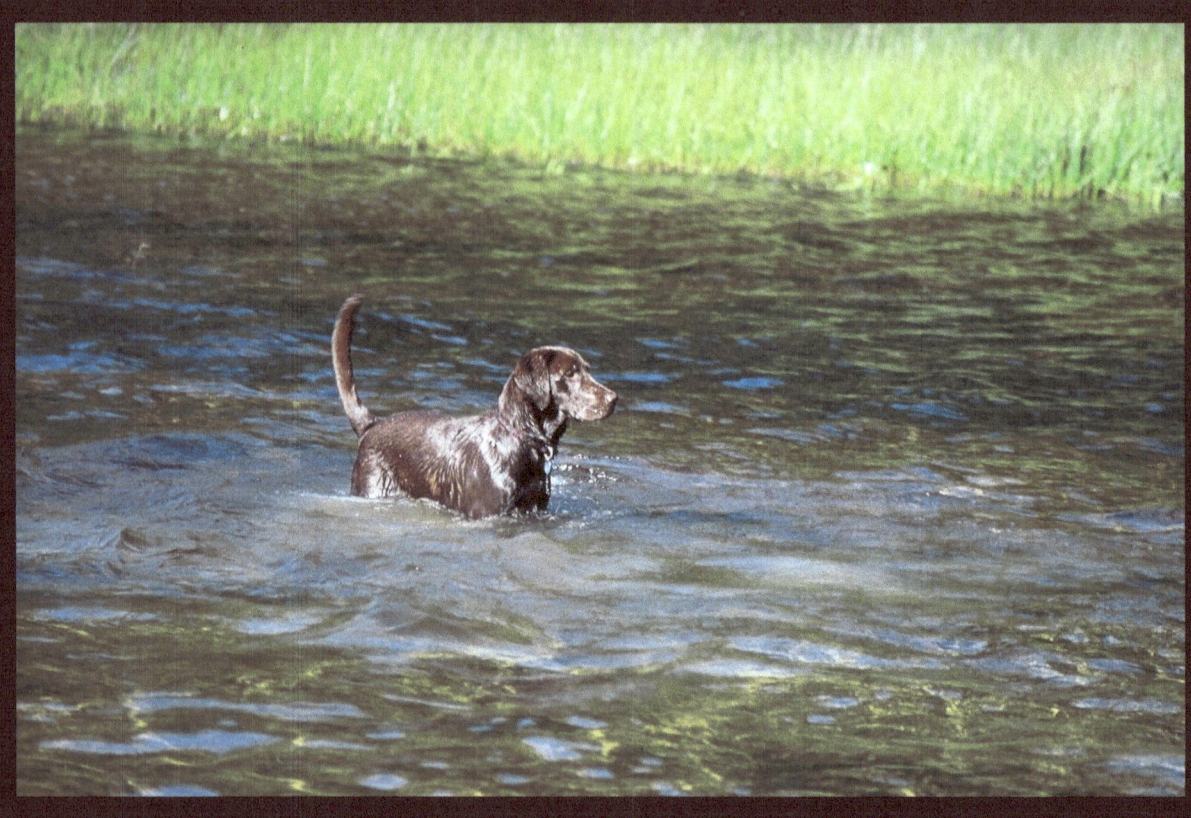

Here a fish. There a fish. Everywhere a … duck!
#dinner

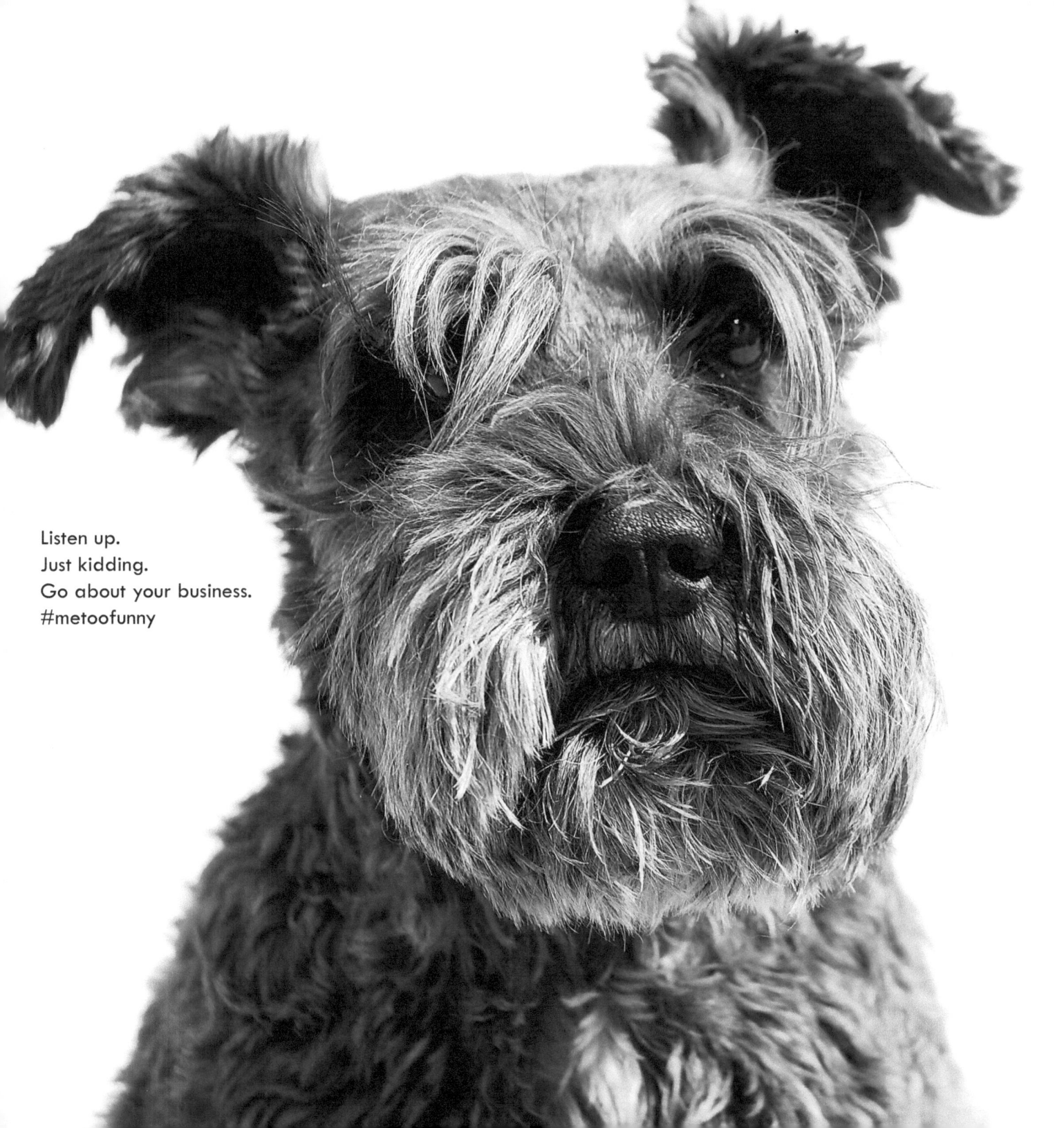

Listen up.
Just kidding.
Go about your business.
#metoofunny

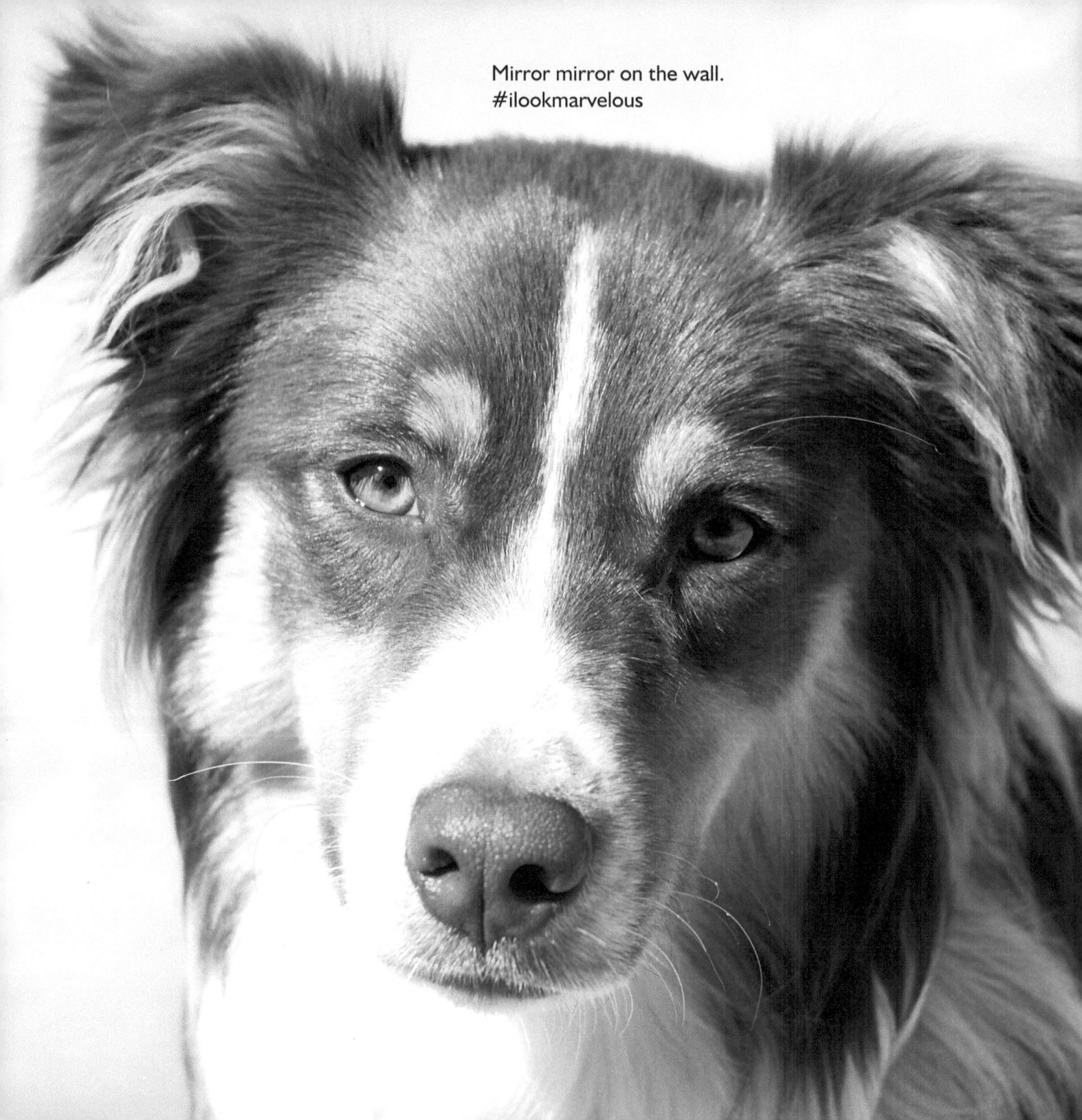

Mirror mirror on the wall.
#ilookmarvelous

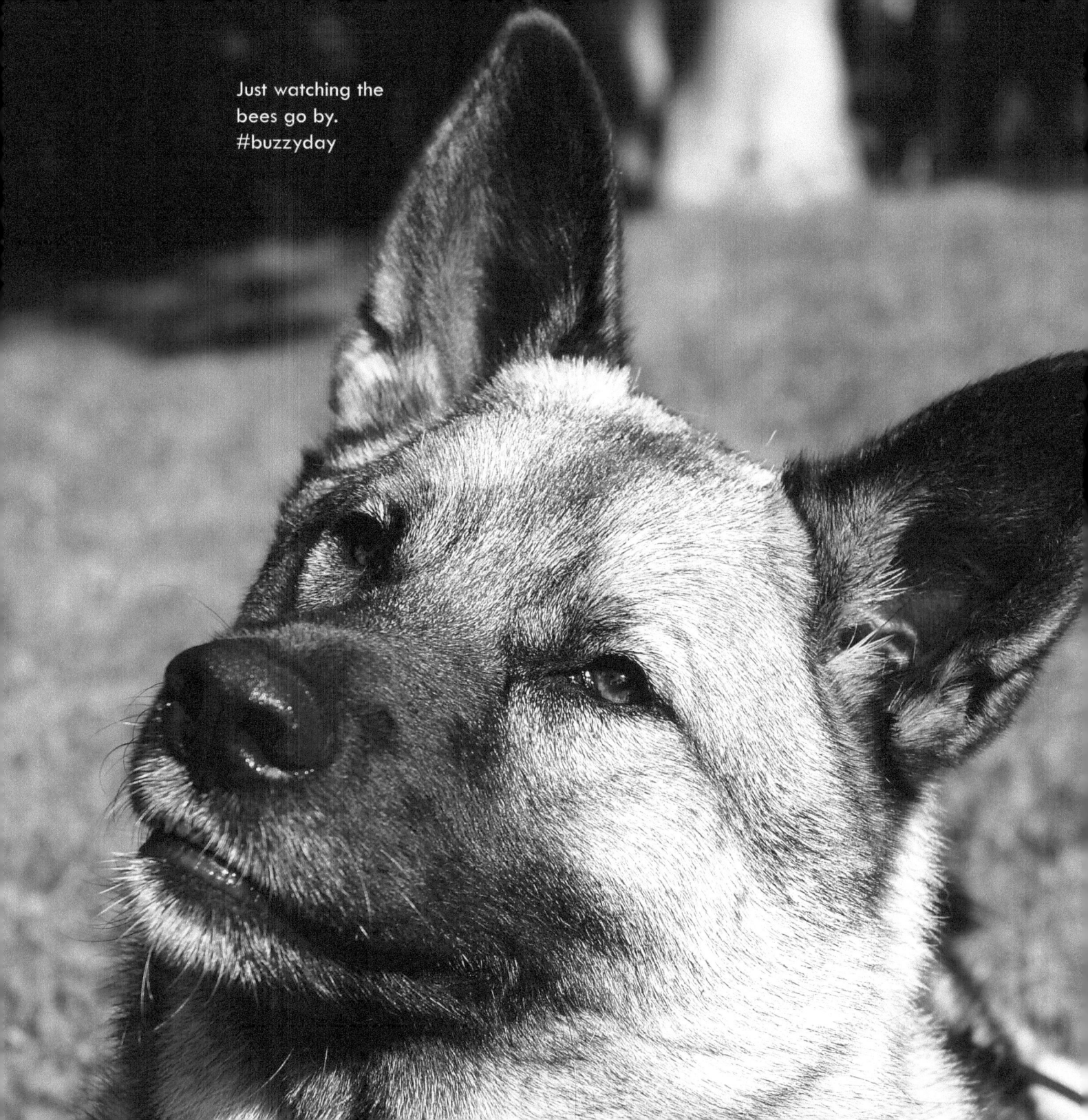

Just watching the
bees go by.
#buzzyday

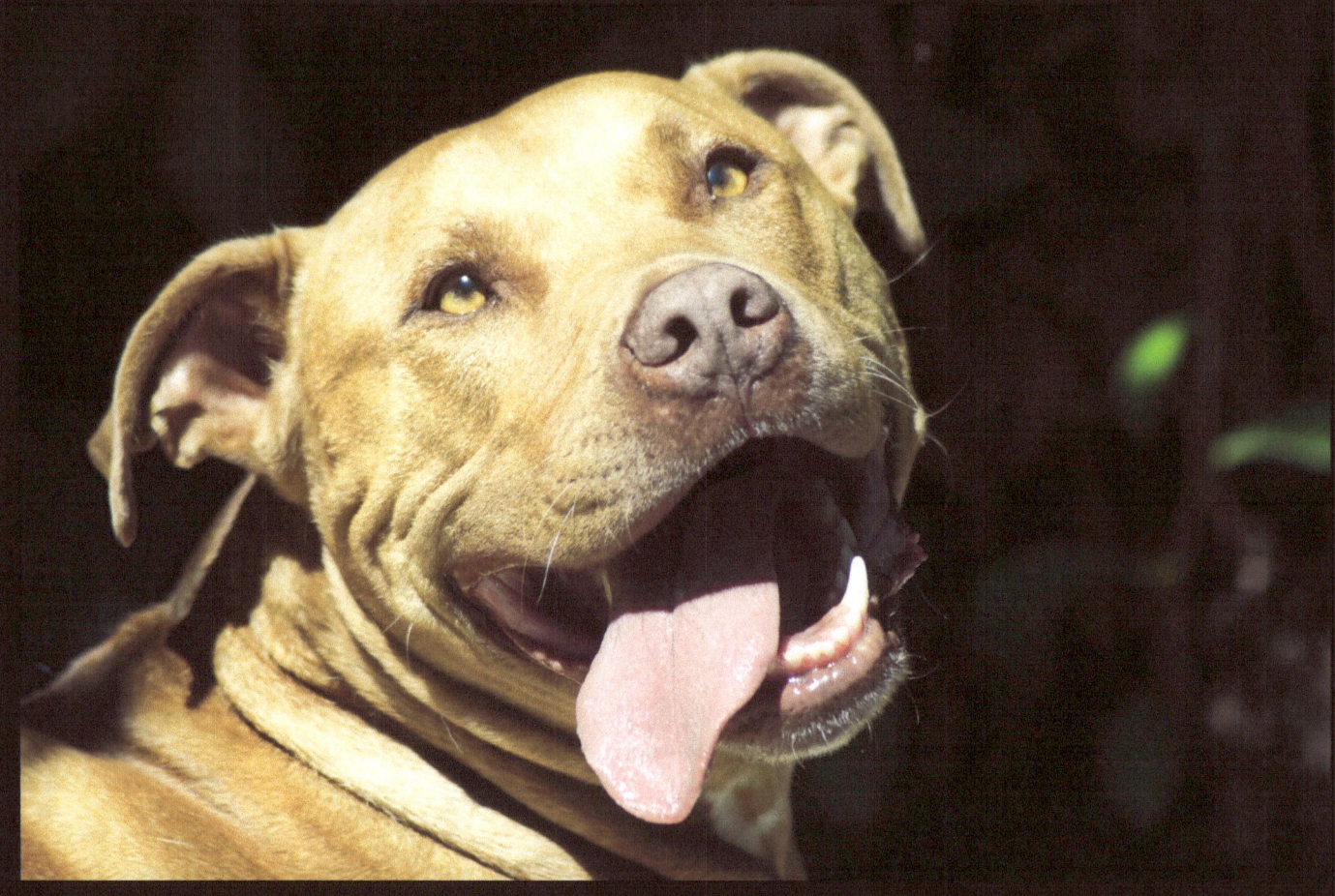

Modeling pose number 2 the "frankly my dear ..."
#rolemodel

I see the chair.
I sit in the chair.
#bethechair

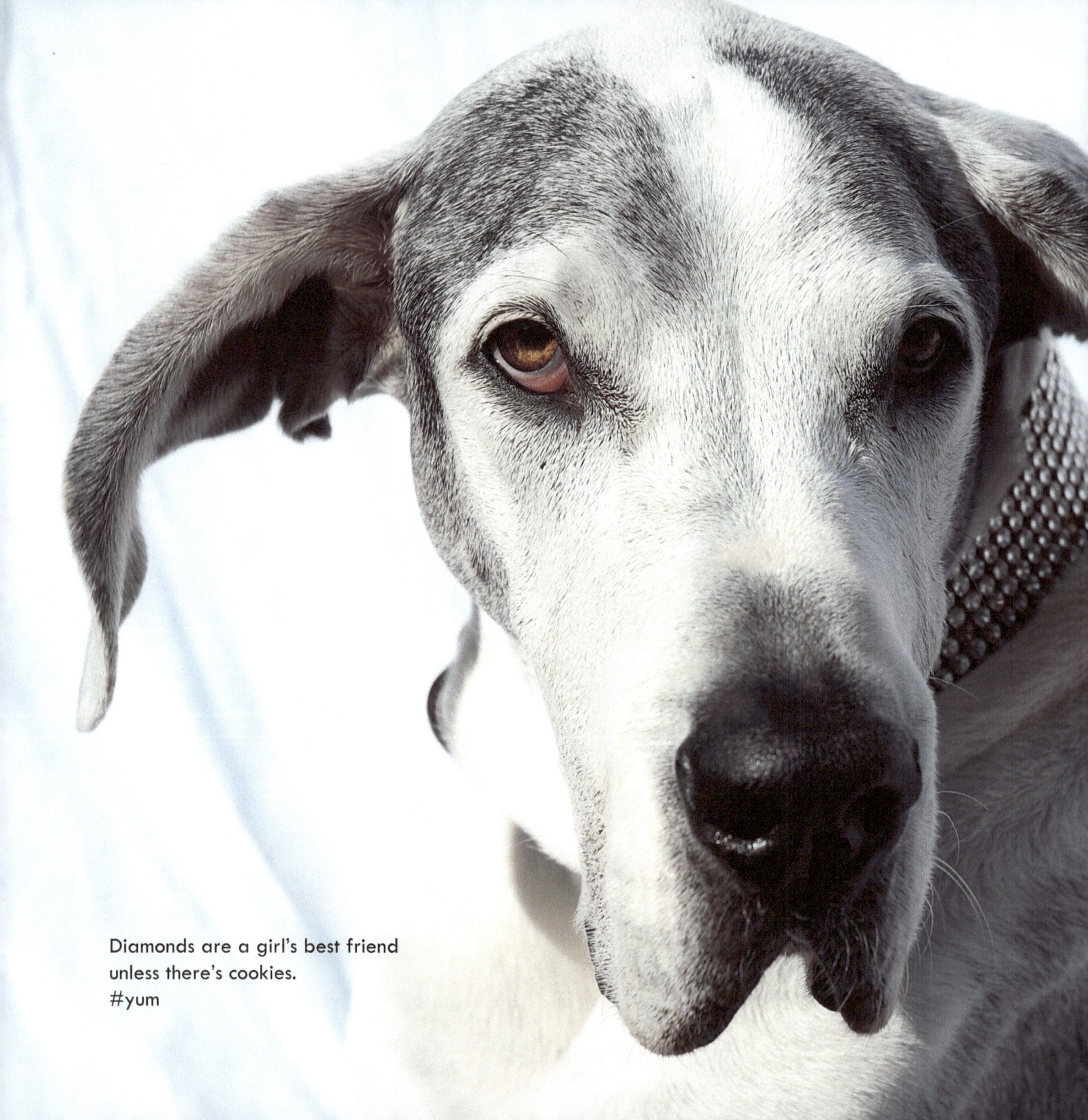

Diamonds are a girl's best friend
unless there's cookies.
#yum

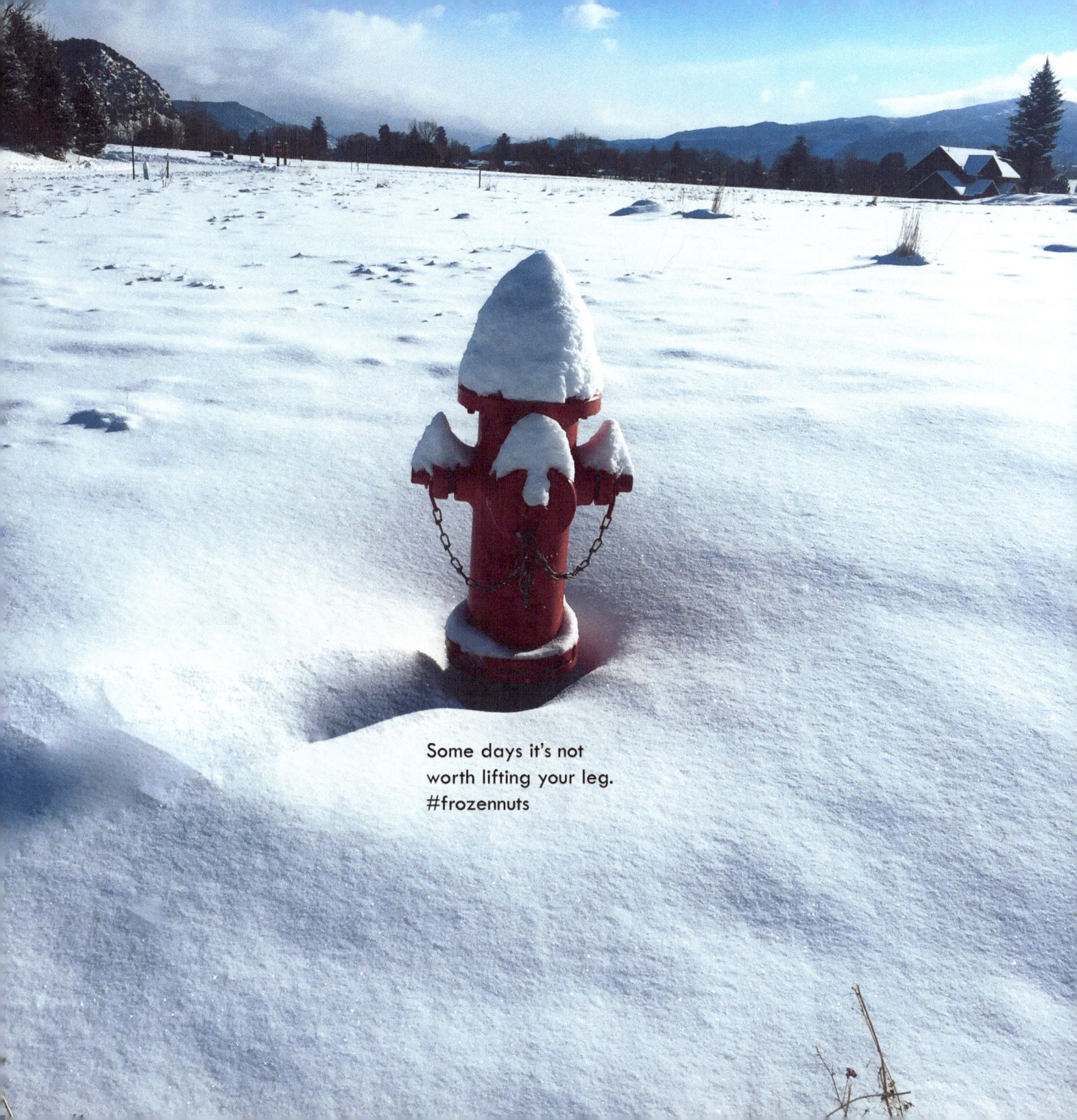

Some days it's not
worth lifting your leg.
#frozennuts

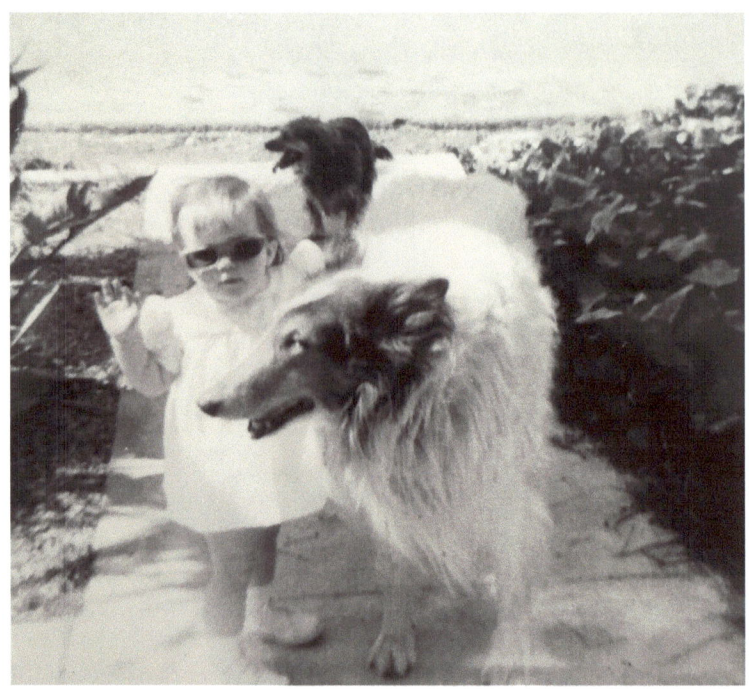

#entourage

Miki Klocke is a professional photographer and fused glass artist. Her images and art can be found at mikiklocke.com.

Follow Miki at: 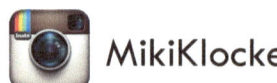 MikiKlocke

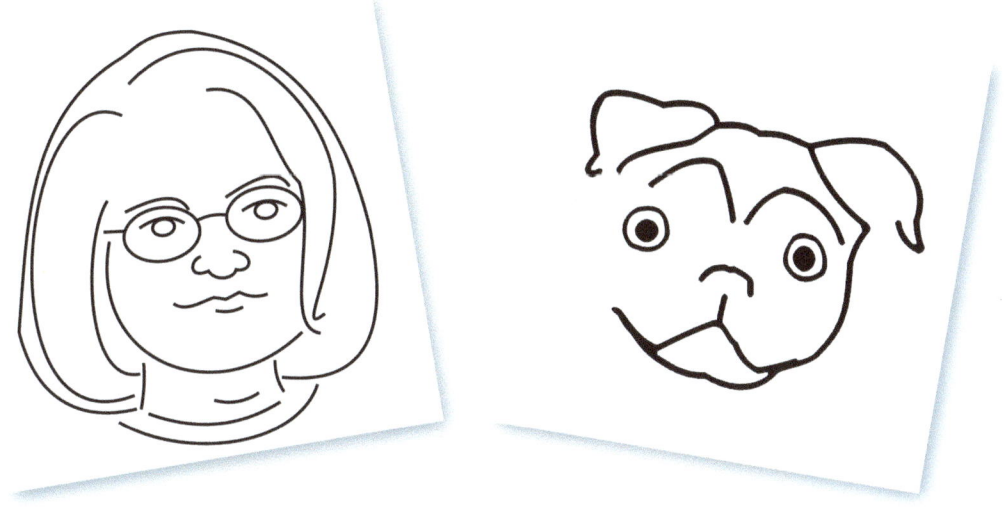

#bestfriendsforever

After attending the Rhode Island School of Design and Art Center College, Mary Ogle emerged with a solid grounding in the art of oil painting. Not satisfied with the limitations of brush and canvas, she stumbled upon the world of computer graphics and never looked back. To see more of Mary's work visit maryogle.com.

Follow Mary at: 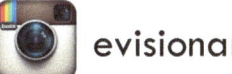 evisionarts

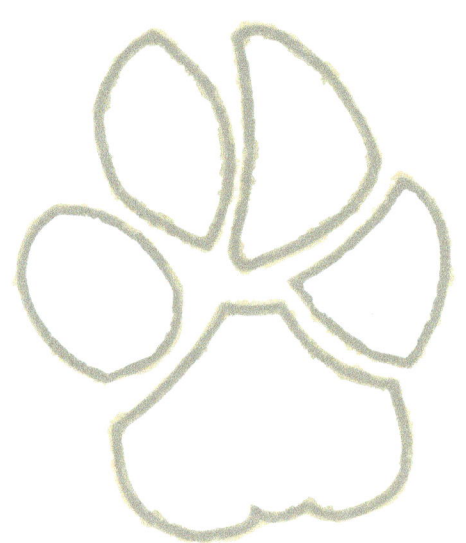

more books by Miki Klocke and Mary Ogle

wordandpicturebook.com

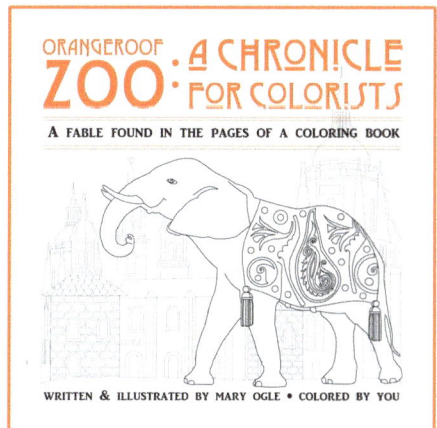

Orangeroof Zoo:
A Coloring Book for Adults
written and illustrated
by Mary Ogle, colored by You
available on Amazon

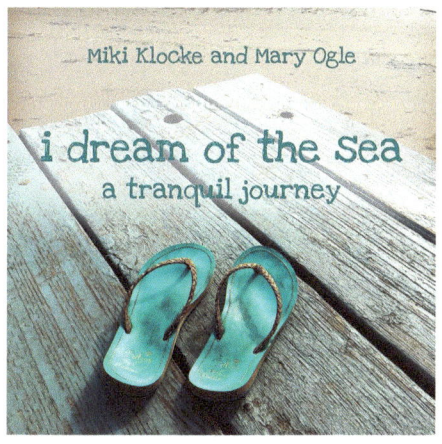

I Dream of the Sea
by Miki Klocke and Mary Ogle
photography by Miki Klocke
illustration by Mary Ogle
available on Amazon

tweets from the cat

tweets from the cat
by Miki Klocke and Mary Ogle
photography by Miki Klocke
illustration by Mary Ogle
coming soon

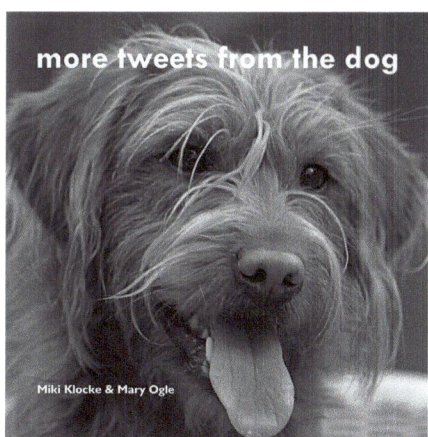

more tweets from the dog
by Miki Klocke and Mary Ogle
photography by Miki Klocke
coming soon

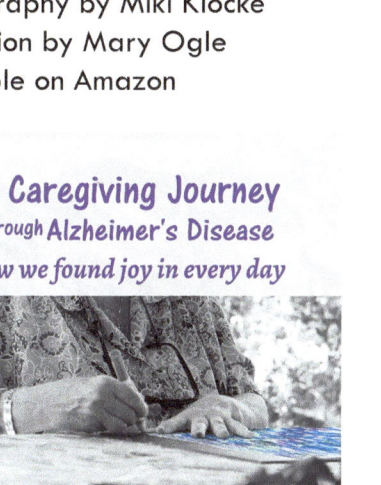

A Caregiving Journey through Alzheimer's Disease
written and photographed by Miki Klocke
art by Janice Klocke
coming soon

www.ingramcontent.com/pod-product-compliance
Lightning Source LLC
Chambersburg PA
CBHW050358180526
45159CB00005B/2071